Step by Step.
Online Marketing Strategy for your Business

Online Marketing Stages - Magic Table

Stage 1	Organic Listing
Stage 2	Activating Social Triggers
Stage 3	Creating Web Home
Stage 4	Activating Web Triggers
Stage 5	Target Inbox
Stage 6	Extra Shots
Stage 7	Make a Deal
Stage 8	The Giant Elephant
Stage 9	Pay The Price
Stage 10	Building Loyal Customer's
Keep Doing it!	

Outline

- Introduction

- Mindset
  - Common types of Brick & Mortar
  - Key elements within a Digital Strategy

- Process to move your Business to Digital World

  - Stage 1: Organic Listing
    - Directory Listing
    - Creating Social Profiles
    - Google My Business

  - Stage 2: Activating Social Triggers
    - Managing Social Profiles
    - Social Groups

  - Stage 3: Creating Digital Home
    - Website
    - Landing Pages
    - Blogs

  - Stage 4: Activating Web Triggers
    - Google Analytics
    - Google Search Console
    - Live Chat Option

  - Stage 5: Target Inbox
    - Email Marketing
    - SMS Marketing
    - Brochure/eBook Free Download
    - Offer and Discounts
    - Newsletters

- Stage 6: Extra Shots
    - Forums
    - Comment Markerting
    - Guest Blogging

- Stage 7: Make a Deal
    - Affiliate Marketing
    - Influencer Marketing

- Stage 8: The Giant Elephant
    - Video Marketing
    - Webinar
    - Podcasting
    - SEO

- Stage 9: Sponsored Ads
    - PPC Ads
    - Display Advertisement
    - Social Media Marketing
    - Video Ads
    - Remarketing/Retargeting Ads

- Stage 10: Building a Loyal Customer's
    - Chatbot Whatsapp/Web
    - Loyalty Programme
    - CRM
    - Personalized Marketing

Introduction

"Brick and mortar" is a term often used to describe traditional, physical businesses that have a physical presence in the form of a physical building or store. The term is derived from the materials used in constructing these buildings: bricks and mortar. These businesses operate in a physical space that customers can visit to make purchases, receive services, or experience products directly.

Here are some key characteristics and aspects of brick and mortar businesses:

Physical Location: Brick and mortar businesses have a physical storefront or location that customers can visit. This location can serve as a hub for customer interactions, product displays, and service delivery.

In-Person Interaction: These businesses allow for face-to-face interactions between customers and employees. This can create a more personalized and human connection, which can be a distinguishing feature compared to online-only businesses.

Tangible Experience: Customers can physically see, touch, try, and experience products before making a purchase. This sensory experience can be a significant factor in influencing buying decisions.

Immediate Gratification: Customers can obtain products or services immediately without waiting for shipping or delivery. This immediate gratification can be especially appealing for certain types of purchases.

Local Presence: Brick and mortar businesses often have a strong local presence, contributing to the local economy and fostering a sense of community.

Operating Costs: These businesses may have higher operating costs due to expenses related to rent, utilities, and maintaining the physical storefront.

Challenges: Brick and mortar businesses face challenges such as competition from online retailers, changing consumer behaviors, and the need to adapt to digital trends to remain relevant.

Omni-Channel Approach: Many brick and mortar businesses are adopting an omni-channel approach, combining physical and digital strategies.

This might involve having an online presence, offering click-and-collect options, or integrating digital technologies into the in-store experience.

Customer Experience: Providing exceptional customer service and a welcoming atmosphere are key components of the brick and mortar business model, as they contribute to customer loyalty and repeat business.

Adaptation: To thrive in the modern business landscape, brick and mortar businesses often need to adapt by embracing digital technologies, expanding their online presence, and finding innovative ways to engage customers both in-store and online.

While online shopping and e-commerce have grown significantly, brick and mortar businesses still hold a valuable place in retail and service industries, offering unique benefits and experiences that cannot be replicated solely through digital channels.

Mindset

The mindset of a brick and mortar business owner often includes aspects such as a focus on customer service, creating a welcoming in-person experience, managing inventory and employees, dealing with local regulations, and adapting to changing market trends.

They may also prioritize building a loyal customer base and cultivating a strong community presence. Additionally, brick and mortar business owners need to be resourceful and adaptive in order to compete with online retailers and stay relevant in the evolving retail landscape.

Common Types of Brick & Mortar:

There are numerous types of brick and mortar businesses across various industries. Some common types include:

Retail Stores: These include clothing stores, electronics shops, bookstores, and other stores that sell physical products to customers.

Restaurants and Cafes: Establishments that offer food and beverages for on-site consumption.

Service-Based Businesses: This category includes hair salons, spas, fitness centers, and other businesses that provide services to customers in person.

Healthcare Facilities: Hospitals, clinics, pharmacies, and medical practices that offer in-person medical services.

Entertainment Venues: Movie theaters, amusement parks, arcades, and other places where people gather for entertainment.

Financial Institutions: Banks, credit unions, and other financial service providers with physical branches.

Automotive Shops: Car dealerships, repair garages, and auto parts stores.

Grocery Stores: Supermarkets and grocery stores where people purchase food and household items.

Home Improvement Stores: Hardware stores, lumberyards, and other stores that provide materials for home improvement and construction.

Specialty Shops: Boutiques, art galleries, and niche stores that cater to specific interests or hobbies.

Education Centers: Schools, training centers, and tutoring services that offer in-person educational experiences.

Hotels and Lodging: Accommodation establishments where travelers stay during their visits.

Businesses can indeed fail if they do not adapt to digital platforms. In the modern business landscape, digital platforms have become a crucial avenue for reaching customers, conducting transactions, and staying competitive.

In today's rapidly changing business landscape, embracing digital platforms is often essential for remaining competitive, reaching new customers, and adapting to evolving consumer preferences. Businesses that fail to do so risk losing market share, profitability, and even the viability of their operations.

Here are some reasons why this can happen:

Changing Consumer Behavior: As more consumers turn to online shopping and digital platforms for convenience, businesses that don't have an online presence can miss out on a significant portion of potential customers.

Wider Reach: Digital platforms enable businesses to reach a global audience, whereas a physical location is limited by its geographic reach. Failing to tap into this broader market can hinder growth opportunities.

Competitive Landscape: Businesses that don't embrace digital platforms may lose out to competitors who do. Online retailers often have lower overhead costs, which can lead to competitive pricing and better customer experiences.

Convenience: Online platforms offer convenience through 24/7 availability, easy product comparison, and streamlined purchasing processes. Businesses without an online presence can't provide these advantages.

Reduced Overhead: Physical stores require expenses like rent, utilities, and staffing. An online presence can significantly reduce these costs and improve overall profitability.

Data Utilization: Digital platforms offer data collection and analysis capabilities that help businesses understand customer preferences, behaviors, and trends. This data-driven insight is crucial for making informed business decisions.

Marketing Opportunities: Digital marketing allows for targeted advertising, personalized messaging, and direct engagement with customers. Businesses without a digital presence miss out on these effective marketing strategies.

Customer Expectations: Modern consumers expect businesses to have an online presence for information, customer support, and engagement. Not meeting these expectations can lead to a negative perception of the business.

Innovation: Digital platforms enable innovation in product offerings, service delivery, and customer experiences. Businesses that stick to traditional methods may become stagnant and fail to evolve.

Crisis Resilience: The COVID-19 pandemic highlighted the importance of digital platforms for business continuity. Those without an online presence struggled to adapt to lockdowns and changing consumer behaviors.

Evolving Trends: Emerging technologies like mobile apps, social media, and e-commerce platforms continue to shape how customers interact with businesses. Ignoring these trends can lead to irrelevance.

Accessibility: Digital platforms make products and services accessible to a wider range of people, including those with disabilities or limitations that affect their ability to visit physical stores.

Several established businesses have faced losses due to their failure to adapt to digital media and changing consumer behaviors. Here are a few examples:

Blockbuster: Blockbuster, once a prominent video rental chain, failed to embrace digital streaming and online rentals. This led to their decline and eventual bankruptcy as competitors like Netflix gained popularity.

Kodak: Kodak, a company known for its dominance in the film and photography industry, struggled to adapt to the digital photography revolution. They missed the shift to digital cameras and online photo sharing, which contributed to their decline.

Borders: Borders, a bookstore chain, struggled to compete with online retailers like Amazon and failed to effectively transition to digital book sales. This resulted in their bankruptcy and eventual closure of stores.

Toys "R" Us: The toy retailer faced challenges from online competitors and e-commerce giants like Amazon. Their inability to establish a strong online presence and adapt to changing consumer preferences contributed to their financial troubles and eventual closure.

RadioShack: RadioShack, a chain of electronics retail stores, struggled to adapt to the changing electronics market and the rise of online shopping. Their failure to pivot and connect with modern tech-savvy consumers led to financial difficulties.

Nokia: Once a leader in the mobile phone industry, Nokia lost ground due to their slow response to the smartphone revolution. They initially underestimated the importance of touchscreens and app ecosystems, allowing competitors like Apple and Android manufacturers to surpass them.

These examples highlight the importance of adapting to digital media and changing consumer behaviors in order to remain competitive in today's rapidly evolving business landscape.

Transforming a brick and mortar business to a digital one can be both challenging and rewarding.

The degree of difficulty depends on several factors, including the nature of the business, the complexity of operations, the industry, and the willingness of the business owner to adapt.

A digital strategy is a comprehensive plan that outlines how a business will leverage digital technologies and platforms to achieve its goals and objectives. It's a roadmap that guides the integration of digital tools and processes into various aspects of the business to improve efficiency, customer engagement, and overall performance.

Key elements within a digital strategy:

Business Goals and Objectives:

Clearly define the business's short-term and long-term goals. These could include increasing sales, expanding market reach, enhancing customer experience, or improving operational efficiency.

Target Audience:

Identify and understand your target audience segments. This involves analyzing their demographics, preferences, behaviors, and needs to tailor your digital efforts accordingly.

Brand guidelines

also known as brand style guidelines or brand standards, are a set of rules and recommendations that define how a brand should be represented visually and communicated consistently across various platforms and materials.

These guidelines ensure that a brand's identity remains cohesive, recognizable, and aligned with its core values and messaging.

Competitor analysis

is the process of evaluating and understanding your business's competitors in order to gain insights into their strengths, weaknesses, strategies, and market positioning.

This analysis helps you make informed decisions, refine your business strategy, and identify opportunities for growth.

Process to move your Business from Brick Mortar to **Digital World.**

Stage 1: Organic Listing

1.a. Directory Listing

A directory listing refers to the inclusion of a business or website in an online directory or listing platform. These directories are websites or databases that categorize and organize information about businesses, websites, or individuals based on specific criteria, such as industry, location, or service offerings. Directory listings provide users with a convenient way to search for and find relevant businesses, services, or websites in a specific area or category.

Directory listings typically include essential information about the listed entity, such as:

Business Name: The name of the business or website.

Contact Information: Contact details like phone numbers, email addresses, and physical addresses.

Description: A brief description of the business or website, highlighting its products, services, or offerings.

Website URL: The web address of the business or website, if applicable.

Category or Industry: The industry or category to which the business belongs (e.g., restaurants, hotels, lawyers, etc.).

Location: The physical location or service area of the business, including the address and geographical coordinates.

Reviews and Ratings: User-generated reviews and ratings that provide feedback on the quality of the business or website's products or services.

Operating Hours: Information about when the business is open or available.

Directory listings serve several purposes, including:

Online Visibility: They help businesses and websites become more discoverable on the internet, improving their online presence.

Local Search: For businesses with physical locations, directory listings are crucial for local search engine optimization (Local SEO) and attracting local customers.

Credibility: Being listed in reputable directories can enhance a business's credibility and trustworthiness.

Marketing: Directory listings can be part of a broader online marketing strategy, helping businesses reach a wider audience.

Common examples of online directories include Sulekha and Yellow Pages

1.b. Creating Social Profiles

Making accounts on different social media sites, such Facebook, Instagram, LinkedIn, and others, is referred to as creating social profiles. In the digital sphere, these profiles stand in for people, companies, organisations, or other entities. Providing personal or business details, like name, email address, phone number, and profile image, is a common step in creating social media profiles.

<u>How It Can Help Your Brand?</u>

- There are millions of active users on social networking networks. A brand can reach a large audience through presence building that may not be possible through other channels.

- Shareable and interesting content has the potential to go viral and quickly promote brand awareness on social media.

- Brands and their audience can communicate directly. Reactions to messages, comments, and feedback help to build trust and a sense of community.

- With social media analytics, brands may learn a lot about their audience. Enhancements to products and services as well as market research can be conducted using this data.

- Brands may reach particular demographics, geographic areas, and hobbies with the help of customised advertising available on most social media sites. This accuracy aids in optimising the effect of marketing expenditures.

- Posts on social media can increase traffic to a brand's blog, website, or online store, which could lead to a rise in sales and conversions.

- Keeping an eye on rival brands' social media accounts helps a business remain inventive and competitive by giving insights into their tactics.

- Likes, shares, and comments are examples of social signals that might indirectly affect a website's search engine ranking, possibly increasing the website's visibility.

How To Do It?

1. Define Your Goals: Decide what you hope to accomplish with social media.

2. Identify Your Target Audience: Recognize the hobbies, demographics, and internet habits of your target market.

3. Choose the Right Platforms: Choose social media channels with the highest activity levels among your target market. For instance, Twitter, Instagram, and Facebook

4. Optimise Your Profiles: Include a clear profile photo, an engaging bio or description, contact details, and links to your website or other pertinent pages in each of your profiles. To strengthen brand identity, use standardised branding components on all social media channels, such as taglines, logos, and color palettes.

5. Develop a Content Strategy: Prepare your content ahead of time. Make a content calendar that outlines the kinds of material you will publish when. Focus on producing content that speaks to your audience that is interesting, worthwhile, and shareable. Videos and other visual items frequently perform better. Make a superb visual investment that complements your business image.

6. Engage Your Audience: Interact with your audience by promptly answering messages, comments, and mentions.

7. Monitor and Adjust: Observe your social media performance on a regular basis.

8. Stay Authentic: Being genuine is essential to fostering trust. In your interactions, be sincere.

1.c. Google My Business

Businesses and organisations can manage their online presence across Google's many platforms, such as Google Maps and Search, by utilising Google My Business which is a free online tool offered by Google. Businesses may give prospective clients vital information about themselves, like their address, phone number, website, business hours, and customer reviews, by creating and validating a Google My Business listing.

How It Can Help Your Brand?

- Your chances of showing up on Google Maps and in local search results are increased when you have a Google My Business listing. Potential clients will find your company more easily when they're looking for goods or services linked to your sector thanks to your enhanced visibility.

- Establishing and maintaining a Google My Business listing enhances the trustworthiness of your company. Consumers are more likely to believe companies that show up on Google since it suggests reliability and authenticity.

- You may communicate with customers by replying to reviews, addressing inquiries, and sharing updates about your goods, services, or specials using Google My Business.

- Google My Business offers information into how potential customers discover your listing and the activities they take, such calling, visiting your website, or asking for directions.

- Enhancing your Google My Business profile through optimization might help you with local search engine optimization (SEO).

It contributes to Google's understanding of your company, which may result in better local search engine rankings. For small businesses looking to serve local clients, this is essential.

- By enhancing your Google My Business profile with images and descriptions, you may highlight your goods and services. Your brand image can be improved by using visual content..

How To Do It?

1. Sign in or Create a Google Account: You will need to establish a Google account if you do not already have one. You can sign in using any Google account you may have, including Gmail accounts.

2. Go to Google My Business: Go to the Google My Business page and select "Start Now" or "Manage Now."

3. Enter Your Business Name: Enter the name of your company here. Proceed using the name you entered if your firm is not listed among the choices.

4. Enter Your Business Address: Enter your company's address here. You can also offer your service region if you deliver goods or services to clients in a particular area.

5. Add Your Business Category: Select a category that most accurately sums up your company. This facilitates Google's understanding of your company's mission and target audience.

6. Add Your Contact Information: Put in the phone number and website URL for your company. Verify that this information is current and accurate.

7. Verify Your Business: Google will have to confirm that you are the company's owner. There are other ways to confirm, such as getting a call, sending an email, or getting a postcard delivered to your company address.

8. Optimize Your Profile: Once your profile has been verified, finish it off by adding pictures, a thorough business description, business hours, and any other pertinent details.

9. Regularly Update Your Listing: Make sure your company's information is current. Make sure to update your Google My Business listing if your business's hours or location change.

10. Engage with Customers: In order to establish trust, reply to consumer inquiries and reviews and interact with them.

11. Utilize Additional Features: Make use of extra features such as sharing news about your company, providing special offers, and updating your posts.

Stage 2: Activating Social Triggers

2.a. Managing Social Profiles

Keeping an eye on and upholding your organisation's social media presence is known as "managing social profiles." It includes producing, selecting, and disseminating information in addition to interacting with viewers, keeping an eye on conversations, and evaluating the effectiveness of social media campaigns.

How It Can Help Your Brand?

- A strong social media presence increases brand exposure. Users can see and share engaging material on social media networks, which raises awareness of your brand.

- It can raise brand awareness, giving them a better chance of connecting with prospective clients and building recognition.

- Companies may interact with clients face-to-face, answer their questions, and deliver first-rate customer care while forging close bonds with their target market.

- A company's credibility and dependability can be increased by a robust social media presence, which also encourages customers to interact with the brand.

- It provides opportunities for alliances, teamwork, and influencer marketing, broadening the company's customer base.

- Social media usage has the ability to enhance website traffic, sales, and conversions.

- Businesses can benefit from social media monitoring by keeping an eye on rivals and learning about their tactics and client sentiment.

How To Do It?

Managing your social media presence is essential to connecting with the target market for your brand. Gaining traction and building a reputable brand can be achieved by understanding the best practices for managing a company's social media accounts.

Use scheduling tools - Scheduling tools assist you in organizing and strategizing your material. These features allow you to schedule particular times for content to be posted, save time maintaining content, and keep each account consistent with the others.

Provide consistency - Each social media account must share the same information and adhere to the same ideals and principles. Consistency aids in brand maintenance and consumer trust.

Follow trends - Understand what is hot on social media and participate in the trends. This could include making memes, challenge videos, and hashtags.

Recycle content - When the content is still relevant, it is acceptable to reuse postings. This may relieve some of the pressure on social media content makers and provide content with a second chance to touch your audience or be viewed by new members of your audience.

Make daily posts - Try to use social media and interact with your audience on a regular basis. A consistent flow of content keeps social media users intrigued and interested.

Tell stories - Sharing company tales can aid in the creation of relatable content that engages your target audience.

React to controversy - People value socially responsible businesses, therefore participating in conversations and declaring support for causes helps build a brand and a valuable emotional relationship with the audience.

2.b. Social Groups

Social groups are communities or networks of people that share common interests, activities, or ambitions in relation to a specific business, product, or industry. These groups can exist both online and offline, and they have a substantial impact on customer behavior, market trends, and corporate tactics. Customers, employees, suppliers, investors, and other business partners are all examples of stakeholders who might be included in social groups.

How It Can Benefit Your Brand

- Social groups provide a platform for customers to express their opinions, feedback, and preferences directly. This information is invaluable for product improvement.

- Businesses can spot developing trends and changing customer preferences by monitoring talks within social groups, allowing them to change their strategy accordingly.

- Social groups help to create a sense of community around a certain business or product.

- Social groups can be used to generate ideas for new products or features.
- Peer-to-peer support, in which customers assist one another with common concerns, can be facilitated by social groups.

- Businesses can adjust their marketing messaging to individual social groups' debates and interests, resulting in a more personalized approach.

- Networking opportunities are facilitated by business-focused social clubs.

- Monitoring social groups enables organizations to notice and respond to unfavorable feedback quickly, reducing possible PR difficulties.

How To Do It?

1. Identify Your Social Groups: Determine which social groupings are important to your company. Existing online forums, social media groups, or professional networks linked to your industry, products, or services could be used.

2. Listen and Learn: Spend time learning the social groups' tone, subjects, and attitudes. Pay attention to what members are saying to determine their wants and concerns.

3. Participate Authentically: Engage in genuine community engagement.

4. Provide Value: Provide insights, advice, and expertise about your business or product.

5. Facilitate Discussions: Encourage debate by asking open-ended questions about your industry or products.

6. Acknowledge and Appreciate: Recognize and thank group members for their significant efforts.

7. Implement Feedback: Consider integrating opinions or ideas from social group members where possible.

8. Measure and Adapt: Analytical tools can be used to assess the effectiveness of your engagement activities. Adapt your engagement strategies based on the data.

9. Educate and Inform: Organize instructional sessions or webinars for the social groups.

10. Maintain Consistency: Consistency is essential. Maintain a strong presence by regularly participating in conversations and engaging with community members.

Stage 3: Creating Web Home

3.a. Website

A website is a collection of publicly accessible, interlinked web pages that share a single domain name. Websites can be created and maintained by individuals, groups, businesses, or organizations to serve a variety of purposes, such as providing information, selling products or services, or sharing personal content.

How It Can Benefit Your Brand

- Online Presence: A website establishes your brand's online presence, making it accessible to a global audience 24/7.

- Credibility and Trust: A professional-looking website can enhance your brand's credibility and foster trust among potential customers.

- Marketing and Promotion: Your website serves as a platform to promote your products, services, and content through various online marketing strategies like SEO, social media marketing, and email campaigns.

- Customer Engagement: A website allows for interaction with your audience through blogs, contact forms, forums, and social media integration.

- Sales and Revenue: An e-commerce website can directly contribute to sales and revenue by providing a platform for customers to purchase products or services online.

- Brand Image: Your website reflects your brand's identity, values, and aesthetics, helping to establish a consistent brand image.

- Analytics and Insights: Websites provide valuable data on visitor behavior, helping you make informed decisions to improve your marketing strategies and user experience.

How to Create a Website

1. Define Your Purpose and Goals: Determine what you want to achieve with your website

(e.g., information sharing, online store, portfolio).

2. Choose a Domain Name:
   a. Pick a memorable, relevant, and brand-specific domain name.
   b. Register your domain through a domain registrar (e.g., GoDaddy, Namecheap).

3. Select a Web Hosting Service:
   a. Choose a reliable hosting provider that meets your needs (e.g., Bluehost, SiteGround, WP Engine).
   b. Select the type of hosting (shared, VPS, dedicated, or managed WordPress hosting).

4. Plan Your Website Structure:
   a. Decide on the pages you need (e.g., Home, About, Services, Blog, Contact).
   b. Create a sitemap to outline the structure and navigation.

5. Design Your Website:
   a. Use a website builder (e.g., Wix, Squarespace) or a content management system (CMS) like WordPress.
   b. Select a theme or template that aligns with your brand.
   c. Customize the design to reflect your brand's aesthetics.

6. Develop Your Website:
   a. Add and organize your content (text, images, videos).

b. Install necessary plugins or extensions for added functionality (e.g., SEO, contact forms, e-commerce).

7. Optimize for Search Engines (SEO):
   a. Use SEO best practices to improve your website's visibility on search engines.
   b. Optimize meta tags, headings, content, and images.

8. Test Your Website:
   a. Test your website on different browsers and devices to ensure compatibility and responsiveness.
   b. Check for broken links, loading speed, and overall functionality.

9. Launch Your Website:
   a. Once everything is in place and thoroughly tested, publish your website.
   b. Announce the launch through your marketing channels (e.g., social media, email newsletters).

10. Maintain and Update Your Website:
    a. Regularly update your content and plugins.
    b. Monitor website performance and security.
    c. Analyze visitor data to improve user experience and achieve your goals.

By following these steps, you can create a website that effectively represents your brand and helps you achieve your business objectives.

3.b. Landing Pages

Landing pages are separate web pages designed for marketing or advertising initiatives. They act as targeted entry points, prompting users to take a certain action, such as making a purchase, signing up for a newsletter, or downloading material. To increase conversions, these pages are meticulously developed with convincing components, few distractions, and a clear call to action. Landing pages frequently correspond to the content of the ad or promotional link that drove the visitor there, ensuring a consistent and appropriate user experience. They are widely used in web marketing to acquire leads, collect data, and increase sales by presenting visitors with a tailored and enticing destination.

How It Can Help Your Brand?

- Increased Conversions: Landing pages are geared to convert visitors into customers, subscribers, or leads by offering a focused message and a clear call-to-action, consequently increasing your overall conversion rates.

- Improved Targeting: Landing pages enable you to generate content that is catered to specific audience segments. You can engage your audience more effectively by catering to the specific needs and interests of different populations.

- Enhanced Data Collection: Forms are frequently used on landing pages to collect visitor information. You can create a valuable database for future marketing initiatives, such as tailored email campaigns, by gathering data such as email addresses or preferences.

- Better User Experience: Landing pages provide a streamlined user experience with relevant content and a streamlined design. This favorable interaction has the potential to increase brand perception and consumer happiness.

- Measurable Results: Landing pages are trackable, allowing you to accurately measure the success of your efforts. You may examine metrics such as conversion rates, bounce rates, and user behavior, allowing you to make data-driven decisions to improve your marketing campaigns.

- Brand Consistency: Landing pages may be tailored to reflect the visual identity of your company, ensuring a consistent and unified brand experience. This consistency reinforces your brand image and fosters visitor trust.

- Cost-Effectiveness: Landing pages enhance the return on investment (ROI) for your marketing initiatives by optimizing your ad spend and targeting specific demographics. They reduce waste by directing traffic toward desired actions.

How To Do It?

1. Define Your Goal: Determine whether your landing page's primary goal is to sell a product, collect leads, promote an event, or encourage sign-ups. The content and style of the page will be influenced by your goal.

2. Know Your Audience: Recognize the needs, preferences, and pain points of your target audience.

Customize your messaging to effectively reach them.

3. Craft a Compelling Headline: Create a clear, short, and captivating headline that explains your offer's unique value proposition. Attract guests' attention right away.

4. Write Persuasive Copy: Create succinct and convincing writing that emphasizes the benefits of your product or service. Use persuasion and answer the visitor's concerns. Maintain short, scannable paragraphs.

5. Use Engaging Visuals: Include high-quality photographs, videos, and graphics to help your message stand out. Visitors can be captivated by visual content and gain a better understanding of your service.

6. Design a Clear Call-to-Action (CTA): On your landing page, include a prominent and visually appealing CTA button. Use action-oriented content that clearly communicates what the visitor should do next (e.g., "Get Started," "Claim Your Free Trial").

7. Minimize Distractions: Remove any superfluous navigation links, social networking buttons, or other things that may draw attention away from your CTA. The desired action should be the center of attention.

8. Add Trust Elements: Incorporate testimonials, reviews, trust badges, or security certifications to increase trust. Visitors are reassured and more confident in completing the required action when they encounter trustworthy features.

9. A/B Testing: Experiment with various aspects including headlines, CTAs, colors, and images. Run A/B tests to see which versions perform the best. For best results, use the data to fine-tune your landing page.

10. Monitor and Analyze: Use web analytics tools such as Google Analytics to monitor visitor behavior, conversion rates, and other important information. Analyze the data on a regular basis to identify areas for development and update your landing page accordingly.

3.c. Blogs

A blog is a type of website or a section of a website that contains regularly updated content, typically in the form of written articles or posts. Blogs can cover a wide range of topics, including personal experiences, industry insights, how-to guides, news, and more. Each post is typically displayed in reverse chronological order, with the most recent content appearing first.

How It Can Help Your Brand?

1. **Enhanced Online Presence:**
   - Regularly updated blogs keep your website dynamic and can attract new visitors, increasing your online visibility.

2. **Improved SEO:**
   - Blogs help improve search engine rankings by providing fresh, relevant content. They allow you to target specific keywords and answer common queries.

3. **Establishing Authority:**
   - By sharing your expertise and insights, blogs can position you as an authority in your industry or niche.

4. **Audience Engagement:**
   - Blogs provide a platform to engage with your audience through comments, shares, and discussions, fostering a sense of community.

5. **Content Marketing:**

- Blogs are a key component of content marketing strategies, helping to generate leads and drive traffic to your website.

6. Customer Education:
   - They allow you to educate your audience about your products, services, or industry, helping potential customers make informed decisions.

7. Building Trust and Relationships:
   - Consistent, high-quality content helps build trust with your audience, establishing a loyal readership and potential customer base.

How To Do It?

1. Choose a Blogging Platform:
   - Use a content management system (CMS) like WordPress, which is user-friendly and widely supported.
   - Alternatively, you can use website builders like Wix, Squarespace, or dedicated blogging platforms like Blogger or Medium.

2. Set Up Your Blog:

- If you're using WordPress, install it on your web hosting server and select a theme that supports blogging.
- Customize your blog's appearance to align with your brand.

3. Plan Your Content:
   - Identify your target audience and determine the topics that will interest them.
   - Create a content calendar to plan and schedule your posts in advance.

4. Write High-Quality Posts:
   - Focus on creating valuable, informative, and engaging content.
   - Use a clear and conversational writing style.
   - Break up text with headings, subheadings, bullet points, and images to improve readability.

5. Optimize for SEO:
   - Use relevant keywords in your titles, headings, and throughout the content.
   - Optimize meta descriptions, tags, and alt text for images.
   - Ensure your content is original and of high quality to avoid penalties from

search engines.

6. Incorporate Multimedia:
   - Enhance your blog posts with images, videos, infographics, and other multimedia elements to make them more engaging.

7. Add Calls to Action (CTAs):
   - Encourage readers to take action, such as subscribing to your newsletter, sharing the post, or leaving comments.

8. Promote Your Blog:
   - Share your blog posts on social media, email newsletters, and other marketing channels to reach a wider audience.
   - Engage with your audience by responding to comments and participating in discussions.

9. Monitor and Analyze Performance:
   - Use tools like Google Analytics to track your blog's performance, including traffic, engagement, and conversion rates.
   - Adjust your content strategy based on the data to improve results.

Stage 4: Activating Web Triggers

4.a. Google Analytics

Google Analytics is a free web analytics service offered by Google that tracks and reports website traffic. It provides detailed insights into how users interact with your website, allowing you to analyze various metrics related to user behavior, website performance, and marketing effectiveness.

How It Can Help Your Brand?

1. Understand Your Audience:
   o Gain insights into the demographics, interests, and behaviors of your website visitors.

2. Track Traffic Sources:
   o Identify where your visitors are coming from (e.g., search engines, social media, direct visits, referrals).

3. Monitor User Behavior:
   o Analyze how users navigate through your site, including which pages they

visit, how long they stay, and their exit points.

4. Measure Marketing Effectiveness:
   - Evaluate the performance of your marketing campaigns (e.g., email, social media, PPC) and identify the most effective channels.

5. Improve SEO and Content Strategy:
   - Discover which keywords and content resonate with your audience and optimize your website accordingly.

6. Set and Track Goals:
   - Define specific goals (e.g., form submissions, downloads, purchases) and track conversions to measure success.

7. Identify and Fix Issues:
   - Detect and resolve issues that may be affecting user experience, such as high bounce rates or slow-loading pages.

8. Analyze Ecommerce Performance:
   - For online stores, track sales, revenue, and other ecommerce metrics to optimize your sales strategy.

How to Set Up and Use Google Analytics?

1. Create a Google Analytics Account:
   - Go to the [Google Analytics](#) website.
   - Sign in with your Google account or create one if you don't have it.
   - Click on "Start measuring" to create a new Google Analytics account.

2. Set Up a Property:
   - Enter your account name and website name.
   - Choose the data sharing settings you prefer.
   - Click "Next" to set up your property (website).

3. Set Up a Data Stream:
   - Select the platform for your property (e.g., Web for a website).
   - Enter your website URL and name.
   - Click "Create Stream" to generate a tracking ID and Global Site Tag (gtag.js).

4. Add the Tracking Code to Your Website:
   - Copy the Global Site Tag provided by Google Analytics.
   - Paste the tracking code into the <head> section of every page on your website. If you're using a CMS like WordPress, you can use a plugin (e.g., Insert Headers and Footers) to add the tracking code

easily.

5. Verify Tracking:
   - After adding the tracking code, return to Google Analytics and click on "Admin."
   - Select "Tracking Info" and then "Tracking Code" to verify if data is being received.

6. Set Up Goals:
   - In the Google Analytics dashboard, go to "Admin" > "View" > "Goals."
   - Click on "New Goal" and follow the prompts to set up goals that align with your business objectives (e.g., newsletter sign-ups, purchases).

7. Link Google Analytics with Other Tools:
   - Integrate Google Analytics with Google Ads, Search Console, and other tools for comprehensive data analysis.
   - Go to "Admin" > "Property" > "Product Linking" to set up integrations.

8. Use Google Analytics Reports:
   - Explore various reports in Google Analytics, such as Audience, Acquisition, Behavior, and Conversions.

- Customize and create dashboards to monitor the metrics that matter most to your business.

4.b. Google Search Console

Google Search Console is a free tool provided by Google that helps website owners monitor, maintain, and troubleshoot their site's presence in Google Search results. It provides insights into how Google views your website and helps you optimize your site for better search performance.

How It Can Help Your Brand?

1. Monitor Website Performance:
    - Track your website's performance in Google Search, including the number of clicks, impressions, click-through rate (CTR), and average position for keywords.

2. Identify and Fix Issues:
    - Detect technical issues such as crawl errors, indexing problems, and mobile usability issues that can affect your site's search performance.

3. Optimize for Keywords:
   - See which search queries bring traffic to your site and identify opportunities to optimize your content for better rankings.

4. Submit Sitemaps:
   - Submit your XML sitemap to help Google crawl and index your site more effectively.

5. Check Backlinks:
   - Analyze the links pointing to your site (backlinks) and ensure they are from reputable sources.

6. Monitor Security Issues:
   - Get alerts for security issues like malware or hacking attempts, and take steps to fix them.

7. Enhance User Experience:
   - Improve mobile usability and core web vitals to provide a better user experience, which can positively impact search rankings.

8. Analyze AMP Pages:
   - Monitor the performance of Accelerated Mobile Pages (AMP) to ensure they are

correctly implemented and performing well.

How to Set Up Google Search Console?

1. Sign Up for Google Search Console:
   - Go to the Google Search Console website.
   - Sign in with your Google account or create one if you don't have it.

2. Add Your Website Property:
   - Click on "Add a property" and enter your website's URL. You have two options:
     - Domain Property: Covers all subdomains and multiple protocols (HTTP, HTTPS).
     - URL Prefix Property: Covers only the specific URL and protocol.
   - Click "Continue."

3. Verify Ownership:
   - Choose a verification method to prove ownership of your site. Options include:
     - HTML File Upload: Download an HTML file provided by Google and upload it to your website's root directory.

- **HTML Tag:** Add a meta tag to your site's `<head>` section.
- **Google Analytics:** Use your existing Google Analytics account to verify ownership.
- **Google Tag Manager:** Use your existing Google Tag Manager account.
- **DNS Record:** Add a DNS TXT or CNAME record to your domain's DNS settings.
  - Follow the instructions for your chosen method and click "Verify."

4. **Submit Your Sitemap:**
   - In the Search Console dashboard, go to "Sitemaps" and enter the URL of your XML sitemap (e.g., https://www.yourwebsite.com/sitemap.xml).
   - Click "Submit" to help Google crawl and index your site more efficiently.

5. **Check for Issues:**
   - Navigate to the "Coverage" report to identify any crawl errors, indexing issues, or pages excluded from search results.

- Go to "Mobile Usability" to check for any mobile-specific issues.

6. Monitor Performance:
   - Use the "Performance" report to track key metrics like clicks, impressions, CTR, and average position for your keywords.
   - Analyze which queries and pages drive the most traffic to your site.

7. Enhance Your Site:
   - Check the "Enhancements" section for reports on Core Web Vitals, mobile usability, and AMP status.
   - Address any issues highlighted to improve user experience and search rankings.

4.c. Live Chat Option

Live chat is a type of customer service that allows website visitors or app users to engage with customer service representatives or support agents in real time. This kind of communication takes place over the internet and allows users to instantaneously ask inquiries, receive advice, or resolve concerns.

Live chat options are often presented in the form of a small chat box on a website or within a mobile app. Users can put their remarks into the chat box, and customer service representatives will answer in real time. Live chat is popular because it gives instant assistance without forcing customers to call or send emails, making it a simple way to acquire quick help or information.

How It Can Help Your Brand?

- Live chat provides real-time assistance, allowing users to receive rapid solutions to their questions or problems.

- You may address the issues that cause cart abandonment by helping customers through the checkout process and closing deals.

- Live chat enables personalized chats, which makes customers feel appreciated and improves their overall satisfaction.

- Quick issue resolution results in satisfied clients, which increases their faith in your company and increases the possibility of repeat business.

- When compared to traditional phone support, the company can handle numerous chat sessions at the same time, making it a more cost-effective way to deliver support.

- Live chat conversations provide significant data about consumer preferences, pain spots, and commonly asked questions, allowing you to personalize your products/services more effectively.

- Efficient support systems contribute to a positive brand image, increasing the likelihood that buyers will pick your brand over competitors.

How To Do It?

1. Choose a Live Chat Software: Investigate and select a live chat software or platform that meets your company's requirements. Consider features like chat customization, tool integration, analytics, and mobile compatibility.

2. Create an Account: Sign up for an account on the chosen live chat platform.

3. Install the Chat Widget: The embed code or plugin can be obtained from the live chat platform. Add a chat widget to your website or mobile app. If you're using a content management system (CMS) like WordPress, this usually entails adding a small code snippet to your site's HTML or installing a plugin/module.

4. Set up Automated Messages: Create automated welcoming messages to greet visitors when they arrive at your website. These messages can start a conversation and direct users to useful resources.

5. Configure Agent Profiles: Members of the team who will manage live chat interactions should be added. Configure agent profiles, including names, photographs, and, if applicable, areas of specialty.

6. Training and Guidelines: Train your live chat representatives on the products/services, FAQs, and customer service policies of your brand.

7. Monitor and Analyze: Monitor live chat interactions on a regular basis to ensure that client inquiries are being addressed effectively. Use the live chat platform's analytics to learn about consumer behavior, common queries, and agent performance.

8. Provide 24/7 Support (Optional): If feasible, offer 24/7 live chat support to cater to customers in different time zones.
Implement chatbots to handle basic queries during non-business hours.

9. Collect Feedback: Seek client input on their live chat experience. Use this input to improve your product and increase client satisfaction.

10. Promote the Live Chat Option: Display the live chat widget prominently on your website so visitors can easily find and initiate conversations.

11. Continuous Improvement: Regularly analyze customer interactions and feedback to identify areas for improvement.

Stage 5: Target Inbox

5.a. Email Marketing

Email marketing is a digital marketing approach that entails sending targeted messages and promotional content via email to a group of subscribers. It is a low-cost and direct approach for businesses to reach out to their target audience, create relationships, and market their products or services. For optimal its impact, email marketing campaigns can include newsletters, special offers, product updates, and event invitations tailored to certain consumer segments.

How It Can Help Your Brand?

- **Direct Communication:** It allows you to communicate directly with your audience by delivering personalized messages and offers directly to their inbox, establishing a sense of exclusivity and loyalty.

- **Targeted Marketing:** You can segment your email list based on demographics, preferences, or purchase activity to ensure that your communications are tailored to each individual receiver. This tailored strategy raises the chances of conversion.

- **Brand Awareness:** Regular, well-designed emails keep your brand in front of your target audience's minds. Consistent communication strengthens the identity of your brand, making it more identifiable and memorable.

- **Customer Engagement:** Emails allow for interactive material such as movies, surveys, and clickable links, which engage customers in a variety of ways. Interactive components improve user experience and boost brand engagement.

- Driving Sales: Email advertising can directly boost sales by using appealing calls-to-action and special offers. Purchases are enticed by limited-time specials and individualized product recommendations.

- Feedback and Insights: Email analytics can provide useful information on open rates, click-through rates, and customer behavior. Analyzing these indicators will provide you with insights into what resonates with your target demographic, allowing you to fine-tune your marketing efforts.

- Building Trust: Emails that are consistent, insightful, and relevant build trust with your readers. By giving value through relevant content, you establish your brand as an industry authority, creating trust and confidence.

- Cost-Effectiveness: Email marketing is less expensive than traditional marketing tactics. It provides a high return on investment and is therefore appropriate for enterprises of all sizes.

How To Do It?

1. Define Your Goals: Determine your goals, such as raising sales, improving website traffic, or increasing brand exposure.

2. Build a Quality Email List: Sign-up forms on your website, social media, or events can be used to collect email addresses.

3. Choose an Email Marketing Service: Use a trustworthy email marketing tool, such as Mailchimp, Constant Contact, or HubSpot.

4. Create Compelling Content: Create information that is both interesting and relevant. Messages should be personalized based on subscriber preferences. In order to increase engagement, include a clear call-to-action (CTA) and make emails visually appealing.

5. Segment Your Audience: Segment your email list depending on demographics, purchase history, or engagement levels. Adapt your messaging to each category to improve relevancy and response rates.

6. Design Responsive Templates: Check that your emails are mobile-friendly. Because many people check their emails on smartphones, your design must

be responsive to different screen sizes for the best user experience.

7. Test and Optimize: To determine what performs best, run A/B testing on subject lines, email copy, CTAs, and send times. Use these information to better future marketing and initiatives.

8. Monitor and Analyze: Monitor open rates, click-through rates, and conversion rates. Analyze this information to determine the effectiveness of your marketing. Recognize trends and modify your plan accordingly.

9. Comply with Regulations: Follow email marketing restrictions such as the CAN-SPAM Act in the United States and the GDPR in Europe. Give subscribers explicit opt-in and opt-out alternatives, and respect their privacy preferences.

10. Nurture Customer Relationships: Use email marketing to establish relationships. Send personalized content, special discounts, and updates to your subscribers to foster a sense of community and loyalty.

5.b. SMS Marketing

SMS marketing, also known as text message marketing, is a marketing approach in which promotional messages or offers are sent to potential and existing clients via SMS (Short Message Service) or text messages on their mobile phones. This marketing approach enables businesses to reach a big audience swiftly and effectively. SMS marketing is frequently used to promote products, services, events, deals, and other business-related information.

How It Can Help Your Brand?

- SMS messages are often read within minutes of receipt, ensuring that your promotional offers, announcements, or alerts are conveyed to your target audience immediately.

- When compared to emails, SMS messages have much greater open rates. This implies that your message is more likely to be viewed by your target audience, increasing the likelihood of engagement.

- SMS marketing enables two-way connection. You might incorporate links to your website, surveys, or special codes to entice customers to interact with your business directly.

- SMS marketing is frequently less expensive than traditional advertising tactics such as print or television advertisements.

- SMS marketing is ideal for publicizing limited-time deals or flash promotions.

- Regular SMS communication can boost client loyalty.

- By advertising items or services, SMS marketing can have a direct impact on sales.

How To Do It?

- Obtain Permission: Ensure that you have the authority to send SMS messages to persons.

- Choose a Reliable SMS Marketing Service Provider:

- Choose a trustworthy SMS marketing service company. These systems include capabilities such as message scheduling, contact management, and campaign effectiveness tracking.

- Segment Your Audience: Segment your audience depending on characteristics such as location, purchasing history, interests, or demographics.

- Craft Clear and Compelling Messages: Keep your messages short, sweet, and to the point. Clearly identify the message's goal, whether it's a promotion, an event invitation, or a critical update.

- Timing Matters: Take into account your audience's time zones. Send messages at appropriate times to prevent disturbing receivers, particularly late at night.

- Personalize Your Messages: When feasible, use the recipient's name and personalize the content. Personalization strengthens the bond between your brand and the customer.

- Include a Clear Opt-Out Option: Always make it simple for recipients to opt out of receiving future messages. This is not only good practice; it is also a legal obligation in many nations.

- Track and Analyze Results: Measure the efficacy of your campaigns using the metrics supplied by your SMS marketing platform.

- Continuous Improvement: Analyze campaign data and apply insights to improve future SMS marketing tactics. A/B testing alternative message styles, timing, and calls to action can provide useful insight into what works best for your target demographic.

5.c. ebook/Brochure Free Download

An eBook/brochure is a digital publication built for electronic devices that conveys information in a visually interesting and interactive manner. It provides a dynamic reading experience on smartphones, tablets, and desktops by combining text, graphics, and multimedia elements. eBooks can be used for a variety of reasons, including educational aids, marketing tools, and narrative platforms.

How It Can Help Your Brand?

- Increased Brand Visibility: Distributing eBooks/brochures online can expand your brand's reach, attracting a wider audience through digital platforms and social media.

- Establishing Authority: High-quality, informative content showcases your expertise, positioning your brand as a thought leader in your industry.

- Lead Generation: eBooks with valuable content can be gated, requiring users to provide their contact details, helping you generate leads, and expand your customer database.

- Cost-Effective Marketing: Compared to traditional print materials, digital eBooks/brochures are cost-effective, allowing you to allocate your budget efficiently.

- Interactive Content: Incorporating multimedia elements and interactive features boosts engagement, ensuring your audience is captivated and more likely to remember your brand.

- SEO Benefits: Optimized eBooks/brochures enhance your website's SEO, increasing visibility on search engines and driving organic traffic to your site.

- Credibility and Trust: Well-researched and professionally designed eBooks/brochures enhance your brand's credibility, fostering trust among your audience.

How To Do It?

1. Define Your Purpose: Determine the purpose of your eBook/brochure (for example, to educate, promote, or entertain). Determine your target audience's special demands or interests.

2. Content Creation: Investigate and collect pertinent information. Create an engaging narrative or structure. Create material that is concise, entertaining, and error-free. Incorporate visuals (pictures, infographics) to improve comprehension.

3. Design and Formatting: Select a suitable layout and format (PDF, ePub, etc.). Use a color scheme and typography that are consistent with your brand identity. Ensure readability across several platforms (desktops, tablets, and cell phones).

4. Interactive Elements: Include multimedia components such as videos, audio samples, and interactive links. Make visually appealing infographics and images to present data or concepts.

5. Professional Tools: For finished layouts, use graphic design software (Adobe InDesign, Canva). Use eBook converters to properly format your work.

6. Engaging Cover: Create an eye-catching cover that accurately conveys the information. Include a

title, subtitle, and eye-catching graphics.

7. Call to Action (CTA): Include CTAs that encourage readers to take specific actions (for example, visit your website or subscribe).

8. Editing and Proofreading: Clarity, coherence, and grammar should all be checked. To avoid mistakes, proofread thoroughly.

9. Distribution: Choose whether to make it available for free or as a paid product. For distribution, use services such as Amazon Kindle, Apple Books, or your own website.

10. Promotion: To market the eBook, use social media, email newsletters, and your website. Collaborate with influencers or bloggers to increase your reach.

11. Gather Feedback: Encourage readers to submit feedback so that future improvements can be made. Analyze reader engagement through analytics tools.
12. Iterate and Improve: Examine the performance of the eBook. Take use of reader comments to inform your future eBook tactics.

5.d. Offer/Discounts

Offers and discounts are marketing methods used by firms to attract clients and increase revenue. These incentives often involve temporarily lowering the price of products or services or delivering extra items or services for free or at a reduced rate. Buy-one-get-one-free deals, percentage-based discounts, cashback offers, and bundled packages are examples of offers. Businesses utilize these campaigns to instill a sense of urgency in their clients, prompting them to make rapid purchases.

How It Can Help Your Brand?

- Attract New Customers: Discounts might attract new clients who are price-sensitive and looking for a good deal, hence increasing your customer base.

- Increase Sales: Offers instill a sense of urgency in clients, driving them to make purchases they might have put off, resulting in greater sales revenue.

- Clear Inventory: Discounts aid in the clearance of excess inventory, minimizing losses due to obsolete or unsold products, and making a place for new inventory.

- Enhance Brand Loyalty: Regular discounts can foster consumer loyalty, resulting in repeat business and a loyal customer base.

- Competitive Advantage: Offering greater discounts than competitors might provide you a competitive advantage, luring clients away from competitors.

- Boost Brand Awareness: Offers that are well-promoted can draw attention, resulting in greater brand visibility and recognition, particularly through word-of-mouth and social media sharing.

- Gather Customer Data: Customers are frequently required to register for offers, which provides significant data for focused marketing efforts and understanding client preferences.

- Promote New Products: Offers can be used to promote new items, generate awareness, and encourage consumer trials.

How To Do It?

- Understand Your Audience: Analyze your consumer base to learn about their preferences, purchasing habits, and what kinds of offers would be most appealing to them.

- Set Clear Objectives: Establish clear objectives for your promotions, such as growing sales, clearing inventory, recruiting new customers, or promoting specific products.

- Choose the Right Type of Offer: Consider incentives like percentage discounts, buy-one-get-one-free deals, cashback deals, or loyalty programs. Choose one that corresponds to your goals and client preferences.

- Set a Budget: Calculate how much you can afford to discount without jeopardizing your profit margins. Your deal should be appealing to clients while remaining financially viable for your company.

- Promote Creatively: To promote your deals, use a variety of marketing platforms, such as social media, email marketing, your website, and, if applicable, physical storefronts. Create appealing communications that emphasize the value that buyers will receive.

- Create a Sense of Urgency: Use phrases like "limited time offer" or "while supplies last" to create urgency, encouraging customers to act quickly.

- Track and Analyze Results: Track the performance of your offers using analytics tools. Keep track of KPIs like increased revenue, website traffic, and customer involvement. Examine the data to determine what worked and what didn't.

- Collect Feedback: Encourage customers to provide feedback on your products and services. This can assist you in better understanding client satisfaction and making improvements for future campaigns.

5.e. Newsletter

A newsletter is a written periodical that communicates with subscribers regularly, generally via email. Newsletters are frequently used to alert readers about news, events, or other information relevant to a specific topic or organization.

Along with promotional emails, several newsletters play a role in digital marketing initiatives. Unlike ordinary marketing emails, which can read like a shopping catalog, customized newsletters frequently include brief articles with important information about the company's products or services as well as its industry.

How It Can Help Your Brand?

- **Direct Communication:** Newsletters allow you to communicate directly with your target audience. Without the use of intermediaries, you can transmit your brand message, promote products or services, and publish updates.

- **Building Relationships:** Sending valuable content to subscribers regularly aids in the development of a trusting and credible relationship. People are more inclined to stay loyal to your brand if they think your mailings are helpful and entertaining.

- **Brand Awareness:** Newsletters help your readers remember your brand. Consistent communication contributes to the reinforcement of your brand's identity, making it more identifiable. This greater visibility may result in increased brand recall.

- **Driving Traffic:** Newsletters can help attract visitors to your website, blog, or social media platforms. You encourage subscribers to visit your site, investigate your items, and interact with your brand by offering connections to your online presence.

- Promoting Products/Services: Newsletters can be used to market new products, services, or special offers. Subscriber-only promotions can generate a sense of exclusivity, prompting customers to make purchases.

- Educating Your Audience: Newsletters enable you to inform your readers about your industry, products, or services. By giving useful content, you establish your brand as an authority in your sector, increasing subscriber confidence.

- Gathering Feedback: Newsletters can be used to seek input from your target audience. Newsletter surveys or polls can assist you in learning client preferences, allowing you to adjust your products accordingly.

- Analytics and Improvement: You can track open rates, click-through rates, and subscriber behavior with email marketing platforms that provide granular statistics. By studying this data, you may improve your mailing content and strategy.

- Boosting Sales: Finally, engaging newsletters that provide value and relevance might result in greater sales. Newsletters can help your bottom line, whether through direct sales offers or lead nurturing.

How To Do It?

- Define Your Goals: Determine the purpose of your newsletter. Is it to drive sales, increase website traffic, or provide valuable content to your audience?

- Choose an Email Marketing Service: Select an email marketing platform like Mailchimp, Constant Contact, or HubSpot.

- Build Your Email List: Urge followers on social media and website visitors to sign up for your newsletter.

- Design Your Newsletter: Utilize the templates that your email marketing provider offers, or create a unique template that captures the essence of your company.

- Create Compelling Content: Write interesting and pertinent articles for your newsletter. Articles, product updates, business news, and exclusive deals are a few examples of this.
- Personalize and Segment: Divide up your email list into segments according to things like interests, past purchases, and location.

- Include Clear Calls-to-Action (CTAs): Tell readers what to do after that. Add compelling calls to action (CTAs) whenever possible, whether they are found on your website, in an article, or during a transaction.

- Comply with Regulations: Make sure your newsletters abide by email marketing laws, such as the GDPR in Europe and the CAN-SPAM Act in the United States.

- Monitor and Analyze: Observe the data that your email marketing tool is providing.

- Engage with Subscribers: Encourage feedback and engagement.

Stage 6: Extra Shots

6.a. Forums

Forums, often known as online discussion boards or message boards, are digital platforms that allow internet users to communicate asynchronously. They give a forum for people to discuss, share information, ask questions, and voice their opinions on a variety of issues. Forums are divided into categories and threads, allowing users to join in discussions about topics of interest to them. Text-based messages, multimedia information, and links can be posted by participants, promoting a sense of community and knowledge exchange. Forums are essential for connecting people with similar interests and providing a forum for meaningful debate and collaboration in the online world.

How It Can Help Your Brand?

- Community Engagement: Participating in industry or specialist forums helps you to interact directly with potential consumers. You may create your brand as an authority on the subject by answering questions, providing helpful insights, and offering solutions.

- Brand Visibility: Actively participating in debates about your products or services raises the visibility of your brand. When visitors perceive your brand name coupled with useful and interesting information, brand awareness improves.

- Market Research: Forums offer an exceptional opportunity to hear client feedback, thoughts, and concerns. Monitoring discussions can assist you in understanding market trends, identifying client needs, and fine-tuning your products or services as needed.

- Networking: Forums enable you to network with other businesses, industry leaders, and potential partners. Building relationships can lead to collaborations, partnerships, and cross-promotional opportunities, thereby broadening the impact of your brand.

- Traffic and SEO: Participating in forums can help boost visitors to your website. When you post useful content or link to relevant sites, you can enhance referral traffic to your website. Furthermore, forum connections might help your website's SEO efforts, increasing your online visibility.

- **Customer Support:** Forums can be used to supplement your customer service. By openly responding to customer questions and complaints, you demonstrate transparency and establish trust among your audience.

- **Content Ideas:** Monitoring forum discussions can provide useful insights into the issues of interest to your audience. This data may be used to inspire blog posts, videos, and other sorts of material, ensuring that your content remains relevant and engaging to your target audience.

How To Do It?

- **Identify Relevant Forums:** Investigate forums about your industry, niche, or target demographic. Choose platforms with an active user base and debates about your products or services.

- **Understand Forum Rules and Guidelines:** Each forum has its own set of norms and rules. Familiarize yourself with these rules to ensure that you engage in accordance with the forum's norms.

- Create a Profile: Register on the chosen forums. Make a descriptive profile with your brand name, a brief description, and a link to your website. A detailed profile gives your interactions more legitimacy.

- Listen and Learn: Spend time observing active debates to gain a better understanding of the forum culture. Learn about the community's interests, the language they speak, and the difficulties they confront. This understanding will enable you to make a meaningful contribution.

- Provide Value: Concentrate on adding value to the conversations. Answer questions, provide solutions, and share your knowledge. Avoid overt self-promotion and instead strive to truly assist people. Indirectly, valuable contributions will automatically boost your brand.

- Be Respectful and Professional: Maintain a professional and respectful tone in all of your dealings. Avoid becoming involved in intense disputes or arguments. Constructive criticism is okay, but it must always be done with courtesy.

- Regular Participation: Engage on a regular basis. Regular engagement keeps your brand on the radar of the community. Be patient; it takes time to create connections and trust.

- Monitor Brand Mentions: Keep an eye out for talks that involve your brand. Address any issues or inquiries as soon as possible. Exhibiting exceptional customer service in public places can help your brand's reputation.

- Use a Signature: Some forums allow you to customize your signature, which shows at the bottom of your postings. Use this field to provide a brief brand tagline and a link to your website or social media profiles.

- Analyze Results: Assess the impact of your forum participation by tracking your website traffic and engagement stats. Analyze which forums provide the most traffic and conversions to better focus your efforts.

6.b. Comment Marketing

Comment marketing is a method in which organizations or individuals interact with their target audience by leaving comments on various online platforms such as blogs, social media posts, forums, and other community-based websites. The purpose of comment marketing is to develop a presence, cultivate relationships, and promote products or services by actively participating in relevant debates and conversations.

How It Can Help Your Brand?

- Increased Visibility: Participating in prominent blogs, social media posts, or forums in your niche can help your brand gain attention.

- Establishing Authority: Thoughtful and informative remarks can establish you and your brand as industry authorities.

- Building Relationships: Commenting on other people's material allows you to interact with your audience directly.

- Driving Traffic: People are more inclined to click on your name/profile if your comments are intelligent and informative, which can drive traffic to your website or social media platforms.

- Networking Opportunities: Comment marketing allows you to network with other pros in your field.

- Understanding Audience: You can learn about your target audience's tastes, viewpoints, and pain concerns by actively participating in internet forums.

- **Improved SEO:** Commenting on relevant blogs and websites might help you gain significant backlinks to your own website.

- **Crisis Management:** Participating in comment sections allows you to immediately address issues or critiques.

- **Feedback and Market Research:** Comments might provide useful information about your products or services.

How To Do It?

- **Identify Relevant Platforms:** Determine which platforms your target audience uses. This could include industry blogs, social media platforms, forums, or community websites.

- **Research and Read:** Spend time on these platforms reading the information and comments. Recognize the audience's subjects, tone, and interests.

- **Create a Genuine Profile:** If the platform requires a user profile, be sure it accurately portrays you or your brand. Use a clear profile picture and provide accurate information about yourself or your business.

- Add Value: When you comment, provide value to the discussion.
- Be Respectful and Positive: Even if you disagree with someone, maintain a respectful demeanor.

- Personalize Your Comments: Personalize your comments according to the material.

- Respond to Responses: If someone responds to your comment, engage in further conversation.

- Avoid Self-Promotion (Most of the Time): While the ultimate goal may be to indirectly promote your company, avoid overt self-promotion. Instead, concentrate on being sincere and helpful. Your knowledge and experience will easily shine through.

- Stay Consistent: Engage with the community on a regular basis. Consistency aids in the development of connections and the establishment of your presence in the community.

- Track Your Efforts: Keep an eye on the influence of your comments. Use web analytics tools to evaluate if your website traffic has increased as a result of your participation on the platforms.

- **Be Patient:** It takes time to establish a reputation and see actual rewards from comment marketing. Be persistent and patient in your endeavors.

- **Adapt and Learn:** Take note of what works. If various types of comments or platforms produce higher results, modify your strategy accordingly. Adjust your plan based on comments.

6.c. Guest Blogging

Guest blogging is a type of content marketing approach in which individuals or businesses write and publish articles on other people's or businesses' websites or blogs. The goal is to attract a larger audience, enhance brand awareness, and create authority in a certain industry or specialty. Guest bloggers generate valuable and relevant content for the audience of the host site, receiving prominence and potential traffic back to their own website. This approach also improves networking opportunities and increases collaboration among members of the online community.

How It Can Help Your Brand?

- Increased Visibility: Guest posts on prominent blogs can increase your brand's visibility and reach by exposing it to a larger audience.
- Enhanced Credibility: Publishing high-quality material on trusted websites elevates your brand as an authority in your area, increasing audience credibility and confidence.

- Targeted Traffic: Guest blogging helps you to reach out to the audience of the host site, resulting in targeted traffic to your website or social media platforms.

- Improved SEO: Backlinks from authoritative websites improve your website's search engine ranking and visibility on search engine results pages (SERPs).

- Networking Opportunities: Guest blogging allows you to connect with other bloggers and influencers, which expands your network and opens the door to collaborations and partnerships.

- Brand Awareness: Engaging content contributes to brand recognition, which ensures that more people know and remember your brand.

- **Content Diversity:** Guest blogging allows you to vary your material and exhibit your skills across multiple platforms, catering to various audience segments.
- **Increased Social Media Followers:** Quality guest posts are frequently shared on social media sites, increasing your brand's followers and engagement.

- **Lead Generation:** Engaging content can pique potential customers' attention, resulting in more leads and conversions for your products or services.

- **Long-term Relationships:** Building relationships with other bloggers and site owners through guest blogging can lead to long-term collaborations, increasing the reach and influence of your business.

How To Do It?

- **Identify Your Goals:** Establish your goals for guest posting. Clarity on your goals is critical when it comes to generating website traffic, building backlinks, or establishing authority.

- Research Relevant Blogs: Determine whether blogs and websites in your niche accept guest posts. Look for platforms with active audiences and a positive reputation.

- Understand the Audience: Investigate the target blog's audience. Personalize your material to their interests, challenges, and preferences. Guest writings should be useful to the readers.

- Create High-Quality Content: Create content that is well-researched, educational, and engaging. Concentrate on providing unique insights, actionable advice, or interesting stories. Originality is essential.

- Pitch Your Ideas: Send a brief and tailored pitch to the blog's owners or editors. Explain why your proposed themes are relevant to their readership and how your post will help their blog.

- Follow Guidelines: If your pitch is accepted, follow the blog's formatting, word count, and style rules. Make sure your content matches the tone and structure of the host blog.

- Include a Bio and Links: Include a brief author bio in your guest post that highlights your expertise and gives a link back to your website or social media networks. This is critical for increasing traffic to your platforms.

- Engage with Readers: Respond to comments on your guest post as soon as possible. Engaging the audience boosts your credibility and motivates readers to visit your website.

- Promote Your Guest Post: Promote your guest post on social media, email newsletters, and other marketing platforms. This broadens its audience and benefits both you and the host blog.

- Maintain Relationships: After your guest article is published, thank the blog owner and keep in touch. Building solid relationships can lead to future guest blogging and collaborative possibilities.

Stage 7: Make A Deal

7.a. Affiliate Marketing

One kind of performance-based marketing is affiliate marketing, where a company pays its affiliates to drive customers or make sales using their marketing efforts. Put differently, affiliates market a business's goods or services on their platforms (websites, blogs, social media accounts, email lists, etc.) in exchange for a commission on each sale, click, lead, or other specific action that comes about as a result of their marketing efforts.

How It Can Help Your Brand?

- Increased Exposure and Reach: Affiliates frequently have a following that they have built. Your brand can reach new and varied audiences with affiliate partnerships that may not have been possible with traditional marketing strategies.

- Cost-Effective Marketing: Affiliates are only compensated for genuine sales or leads they produce. Because of the performance-based model, you're spending in marketing that yields quantifiable results, making it a cost-effective marketing strategy.

- Improved SEO and Online Presence: Affiliates may advertise their products through a variety of internet platforms. These mentions and backlinks can help your SEO, which will raise your brand's exposure and organic search rankings.

- Credibility: boosting testimonials and suggestions from affiliates can help your brand. Increased conversion rates can result from consumers' propensity to believe suggestions from influencers or people they look up to.

- Flexibility and Scalability: You can scale your marketing efforts up or down with affiliate marketing according to your needs. Affiliates are simple to add or remove as your marketing objectives change.

- Partnership Opportunities: Valuable partnerships can arise from affiliate ties. Certain affiliates may develop into long-term collaborators, bringing value to joint marketing campaigns, events, and new product launches in addition to revenue.

- Partnership Opportunities: Beneficial collaborations can result from affiliate ties. Certain affiliates may develop into enduring partners, bringing value not only to sales but also to joint marketing campaigns, events, and new product introductions.

How To Do It?

- Define Your Goals: Establish the goals you have for your affiliate program. Having specific goals will direct your plan, whether it's for improved revenue, lead generation, website traffic, or brand awareness.

- Set Up Your Affiliate Program: Select a software or affiliate marketing platform based on your needs. There are numerous choices, including Amazon Associates, ClickBank, and ShareASale. As an alternative, if you are technically skilled, you can create your own affiliate network.

- Create Affiliate Policies and Terms: Give a clear explanation of your affiliate policy, including commission amounts, timetables for payments, and rules about promotions.

- Recruit Affiliates: Seek out affiliates with audiences that fit your target demographic and who share the same values as your brand.

- Provide Marketing Materials: Provide your affiliates with the banners, product photos, and promotional content they need to succeed in the marketing world.

- Track and Monitor Performance: Utilize the tracking features that your affiliate platform offers to keep an eye on your affiliates' progress.

- Communicate Effectively: Keep lines of communication open with your associates. Inform them regularly about new items, sales, and modifications to your affiliate program.
- Incentivize Your Affiliates: Provide affiliates with performance-based rewards to inspire them.

- Compliance and Regulations: Make sure that the laws and regulations that apply to your affiliate program are followed.

- Optimize and Evolve: Analyze the performance data regularly to find underperforming affiliates and effective techniques.

- Provide Excellent Support: Offer excellent support to your affiliates.

- Evaluate and Scale: Analyze the results of your affiliate program against your objectives regularly.

7.b. Influencers Marketing

Influencer marketing is a strategic method used by brands to work with people who have a sizable and active social media following. These influencers market goods and services to their audience; they are frequently authorities or well-known figures in particular fields. Through the utilization of influencers' authenticity and trustworthiness, companies may expand their client base, increase engagement, and boost revenue. Influencers provide brand-showcasing material that helps their followers relate to and believe the marketing message, which raises brand awareness, credibility, and possible conversions.

<u>How It Can Help Your Brand?</u>

- Influencers can reach a wider and more focused audience and increase brand visibility and awareness since they have loyal followers.

- Customers are more likely to believe recommendations from influencers because they consider them to be reliable sources. This increases their faith in your company and its offerings.

- Influencers have the ability to produce relatable and real material that showcases your business in a way that is real and connects with their audience. This increases the credibility of your marketing message.

- Influencers can increase your brand's visibility on social media by generating high levels of engagement through likes, comments, and shares.

- Influencers can offer in-depth analyses and product demos, assisting prospective buyers in comprehending the characteristics and advantages of your offerings and making well-informed selections about what to buy.

- Influencers frequently cater to a certain demographic or niche, which enables your company to target a suitable audience segment and increase the efficacy of your marketing initiatives.

How To Do It?

- Set Clear Goals: Establish your goals, whether they be to increase sales, drive visitors to your website, or raise brand awareness. You can gauge your campaign's success by setting clear targets.

- Identify Your Target Audience: Determine which influencers to follow whose followers share the same interests and demographics as your target audience. For a collaboration to succeed, relevance is essential.

- Research and Choose Influencers: Seek out influencers who share your brand's aesthetic, have a strong connection to their audience, and have high engagement rates. For niche markets, take into account micro-influencers—those with tiny but very active followings.

- Build Relationships: Reach out to influencers in a formal manner. In your approach, be specific about why you believe they would be a good fit for your business. Show consideration for their time and ingenuity.

- Agree on Terms: Give a clear explanation of the parameters of the cooperation, including payment, deliverables, publishing dates, and content requirements. Make sure everyone agrees to prevent future misunderstandings.

- Create Authentic Content: Give influencers creative latitude as long as the content reflects the principles and messaging of your business. Audiences respond favorably to authenticity, which increases the effectiveness of the promotion.

- Monitor and Engage: Monitor the campaign's performance in real-time. Track data like conversions, website visits, and engagement. Interact with the audience by quickly answering questions and providing remarks.

- Measure and Analyze: Examine the campaign's outcomes about your objectives. Analyze the return on investment (ROI) by taking into account campaign-related indicators such as sales, internet traffic, and engagement rates. Determine what was successful and what needs to be improved.

- Foster Long-Term Relationships: Think about establishing enduring connections with influencers who provide exceptional outcomes. Recurring partnerships can increase brand consistency and adherent loyalty.

- Stay Compliant: Make sure influencers acknowledge their affiliation with your brand following platform and legal rules. Being transparent is essential to keeping the audience's trust.

Stage 8: The Giant Elephant

8.a. Video Marketing

Video marketing is a type of digital marketing approach that entails developing and distributing videos to promote a product, service, or brand. It uses videos to attract, engage, and convert an audience, resulting in increased revenue and brand visibility. Promotional films, product demos, how-to tutorials, testimonials, and other forms of video marketing are all possible.

<u>How It Can Help Your Brand?</u>

- Videos are intrinsically more interesting than text, easily catching and maintaining viewer attention.

- When information is given in video format, people tend to recall it better.

- Videos can clarify complex ideas or concepts, making them easier to understand for the viewer.

- Ideal for effectively showing the features and benefits of products, services, or processes.

- By presenting satisfied consumers, real customer testimonials in video form can help businesses create trust.

- Videos that demonstrate how a product operates can have an impact on purchasing decisions.

- Websites that include videos frequently score higher in search engine results, increasing visibility.

- Engaging videos are shared on social media sites, which increases reach and traffic.

- Videos can elicit emotions, strengthening the bond between the audience and the brand.

- Anyone in the world can watch videos, breaking down geographical borders.

- Videos may be produced on a variety of budgets, making them affordable to both small enterprises and major corporations.

How To Do It?

- Define Your Goals: Determine your goals for your videos (for example, increased sales, brand exposure, website traffic, or customer interaction).

- Know Your Audience: Understand your target audience's demographics, tastes, and difficulties before creating content for them.

- Plan Your Content: Consider several types of videos (for example, product demos, tutorials, testimonials, behind-the-scenes, and storytelling).

- Create High-Quality Videos: For professional-looking videos, invest in high-quality cameras, mics, and lighting. Write a compelling script that communicates your message clearly and concisely.

- Choose the Right Platforms: YouTube is great for a variety of content and has a large user base.

- Optimize for Search Engines: To boost discoverability, include relevant keywords in your video names, descriptions, and tags. To enhance click-through rates, create an eye-catching thumbnail.

- Promote Your Videos: Increase views and engagement by sharing videos with your email subscribers. Share videos on social media and encourage sharing and participation.

- **Engage with Your Audience:** Respond to comments and feedback to interact with viewers.

- **Analyze and Optimize:** Track views, interactions, and other key information using the platforms' analytics tools.

- **Stay Consistent:** Maintain a constant publication schedule to keep your audience interested.

- **Keep Evolving:** Maintain a close eye on video marketing trends and incorporate new tactics and technologies into your campaign.

8.b. Webinar

A webinar, which is an abbreviation for "web seminar," is a live online event that allows participants to connect, share information, and cooperate in real time over the internet. These virtual seminars, which are hosted on webinar platforms, enable remote audiences to attend presentations, workshops, or conversations. Participants can join from any computer, tablet, or smartphone with internet access.

Webinars frequently use multimedia presentations, slideshows, and movies to increase engagement. Attendees can use chat or audio/video interactions to ask questions, vote in polls, and discuss issues with speakers and other participants. Webinars are commonly utilized for corporate meetings, instructional sessions, product demos, and professional development, as they promote convenient, interactive learning experiences.

How It Can Help Your Brand?

- Expert Positioning: Hosting webinars allows you to demonstrate your knowledge of your business or niche. By giving important knowledge and insights, you establish your brand as an authority, garnering trust and credibility from your target audience.

- Increased Brand Awareness: Webinars draw people who are interested in your subject. They become more aware of your brand, its beliefs, and its services as they interact with your material, increasing your reach and visibility.

- Lead Generation: Webinars are a wonderful way to get leads. Participants are normally required to register, which gives you essential contact information.

- **Product or Service Demonstrations:** Webinars provide an interactive platform for displaying your products or services. You can give live demos, answer questions, and address issues, all of which will help potential clients better grasp your services.

- **Engagement and Relationship Building:** Interacting in real-time with your audience builds a sense of community. Answering questions, reacting to comments, and engaging with participants during the webinar and in follow-up messages can help deepen your audience's relationships and loyalty.

- **Market Research:** Polls and surveys can be included in webinars, allowing you to collect useful feedback and insights from your audience. This information can be utilized to improve your products, services, or marketing tactics.

- **Content Repurposing:** Webinars can be recorded and repurposed as blog entries, social media snippets, podcasts, or ebooks. This increases the value of your webinar content and broadens its reach across several platforms.

- Partnerships and Collaborations: Webinars allow you to collaborate with influencers, professionals, or complementary brands.

How To Do It?

1. Define Your Goals: Decide on the goal of your webinar. Do you want to generate leads, raise brand recognition, demonstrate a product, or establish thought leadership? Define your goals clearly.

2. Choose a Webinar Topic: Choose a topic that will appeal to your intended audience. It should be relevant, entertaining, and useful. Solve a problem or solve a prevalent issue that your audience is facing.

3. Select a Webinar Platform: Choose a dependable webinar platform that meets your requirements. Zoom, WebEx, GoToWebinar, and Microsoft Teams are all popular possibilities. Consider issues such as audience size, interaction, and money.

4. Plan Your Content: Make a script or outline for your webinar. Include a captivating introduction, educational material, visuals (slides, movies), interactive components (polls, Q&A sessions), and a compelling conclusion. Keep it brief and focused to keep participants' attention.

5. Promote Your Webinar: Promote your webinar through a variety of media. To contact your target demographic, use email marketing, social media, your website, and industry forums.

6. Prepare Technical Setup: To ensure good audio and video quality, test your equipment, including the microphone, camera, and internet connection. Learn about the capabilities of the webinar platform, including as screen sharing and chat options.

7. Engage Your Audience: Interact with your audience during the webinar. Encourage people to ask questions, vote in polls, and provide comments. To keep attendees engaged, answer questions in real-time and make the session participatory.

8. Follow-Up: Send a thank-you email to attendees following the webinar, including a recording of the webinar and any extra resources provided. Use this chance to nurture prospects, answer unanswered inquiries, and collect feedback via surveys.

9. Evaluate and Improve: Examine data such as attendance rates, levels of engagement, and participant comments. Use this data to evaluate the success of your webinar and find areas for improvement. Learn from each webinar to improve future sessions.

8.c. Podcasting

Podcasting is a digital media that allows you to create and distribute audio or video material over the internet. It enables people and organizations to create serial series on a variety of topics, which consumers may stream or download at their leisure. Podcasts are often accessible via computers, smartphones, or other portable media devices via platforms such as Apple Podcasts, Spotify, and Google Podcasts. Podcasts, unlike traditional radio, provide diverse, on-demand programming ranging from education and news to entertainment and narrative.

How It Can Help Your Brand?

- Brand Awareness: Podcasts enable you to reach a larger audience, hence enhancing brand visibility and awareness. Regular episodes can help to reinforce your brand's identity and values while also making it memorable to listeners.

- Expertise and Authority: You can demonstrate your competence in your subject by hosting a podcast. You position your brand as a thought leader by discussing industry trends, providing insights, and interviewing experts. This increases credibility and trust.

- Engagement and Connection: Podcasts allow you to engage with your audience on a more intimate level. Hearing your voice humanizes your brand, encouraging closeness and trust. Engaging material keeps listeners coming back, resulting in a loyal consumer base.

- Content Marketing: Podcasts are useful content marketing assets. Repurpose podcast content as blog posts, social media snippets, or newsletters to increase your reach and influence across several platforms.

- Monetization: Podcasts can generate cash through sponsorships, adverts, or premium content subscriptions, giving your brand with a long-term revenue stream.

- Networking: Inviting guests or engaging with other podcasters creates opportunities for networking. Through cross-promotion, these relationships can lead to partnerships, collaborations, or improved brand visibility.

- Feedback and Insights: Podcasts stimulate audience involvement and provide direct feedback. Understanding your target audience's preferences and opinions allows you to better adapt your products or services, increasing customer satisfaction.

- SEO Benefits: Podcast transcripts, show notes, and metadata all help with SEO. Optimized content raises your brand's online visibility, making it easier for potential customers to find your products.

How To Do It?

- Define Your Niche: Choose a topic or niche that corresponds to your knowledge and the interests of your target audience. A certain specialization can assist you in attracting a loyal audience.

- Planning: Choose a podcast format: solo episodes, interviews, panel discussions, storytelling, and so on. Next, Plan the structure and substance of your episodes. To ensure a seamless flow, create an outline or script. Determine how frequently you will publish episodes (weekly, biweekly, monthly, etc.).

- Recording Equipment: Purchase a good microphone, headphones, and recording software. Blue Yeti and Audio-Technica AT2020 are examples of popular mics. Editing software such as Audacity (free) or Adobe Audition can be utilized.

- Recording and Editing: Record your episodes in a calm location. Using editing software, remove background noise, pauses, and typos. Enhance the production quality by including intro/outro music and other components.

- Hosting Platform: Select a podcast hosting service such as Libsyn, Podbean, or Anchor. Hosting platforms save your audio files and distribute them to podcast directories (such as Apple Podcasts, Spotify, and Google Podcasts).

- Create Artwork and Branding: Create eye-catching podcast artwork that is representative of your business. Brand recognition is aided by consistent branding throughout episodes.

- Launch and Promotion: Upload your episodes to your platform of choice. Submit your podcast to well-known directories. Apple Podcasts necessitate the use of an Apple ID and a review process. To market your podcast, use social media, your website, and other avenues. Engage your audience and solicit reviews and feedback.

- Consistency and Engagement: To keep your audience interested, release episodes regularly. Build a community around your podcast by interacting with your listeners via social media, emails, or Q&A sessions.

8.d. SEO

SEO, or Search Engine Optimization, is a digital marketing technique that aims to increase the exposure and relevance of a website in search engine results pages (SERPs). It entails improving a website's ranking in search engine algorithms by optimizing numerous factors such as content, keywords, meta tags, and backlinks. The purpose of SEO is to increase organic (unpaid) traffic to a website, thus increasing its online visibility and attracting more potential consumers. SEO experts can enhance websites to fulfill the criteria that search engines use when ranking pages by studying search engine algorithms and user behavior. Effective SEO tactics assist organizations in reaching their target audience, improving user experience, and driving higher conversion rates.

How It Can Help Your Brand?

- Increased Visibility: SEO helps your website rank higher in search engine results, increasing the likelihood of users clicking on your site. This increased visibility implies that your brand is being seen by more individuals.

- Credibility and Trust: Websites on the first page of search results are frequently seen as more reputable and trustworthy. By optimizing your site for search engines, you raise the credibility of your brand, which leads to higher user trust.

- Better User Experience: SEO is improving the structure and content of your website in order to make it more user-friendly. A well-structured, clean, and uncluttered site with high-quality content improves user experience, resulting in increased engagement and brand perception.

- Targeted Traffic: SEO enables you to target certain keywords and phrases related to your company. People are more likely to find your website if they search for these terms. This customized traffic ensures that visitors to your website are really interested in your products or services, improving the chances of conversion.

- Competitive Advantage: If your competitors invest in SEO but you do not, they are more likely to acquire new customers. You may level the playing field and even exceed competitors in search engine rankings by optimizing your site.

- Local Business Exposure: Local SEO tactics for firms with physical locations might help your brand appear in local search results. This is critical for drawing clients in your local area, especially if you own a physical business.

- Insights into Customer Behavior: SEO tools and analytics can provide useful insights into customer behavior, such as the keywords they use, the devices they use to visit your site, and the geographic locations from which they arrive. This data can help you inform your marketing efforts and make sound business decisions.

- Long-Term Strategy: Unlike paid promotion, the advantages of SEO are long-term. When your website ranks well, it can stay there for a long time, offering a steady supply of organic traffic without the ongoing costs associated with paid advertising.

How To Do It?

- Keyword Research: Using tools like Google Keyword Planner or SEMrush, identify suitable keywords and phrases linked to your business. Long-tail keywords (particularly, longer phrases) that indicate user intent should be prioritized.

- On-Page Optimization: You can craft unique titles, meta descriptions, and proper headings (for example: H1, H2, H3, etc), create a perfect URL structure, add multimedia and images, etc.

- Technical SEO:
    - Mobile-Friendliness: Make sure your website is mobile-friendly for users using smartphones and tablets.
    - Website Speed: Optimize pictures, use browser caching, and minimize code to reduce loading times.
    - Secure Website (HTTPS): Secure your website with an SSL certificate to increase trust and ranking.
    - XML Sitemap: To assist search engines in crawling and indexing your site, create and submit an XML sitemap.
    - Robots.txt: To instruct search engine crawlers on which pages to crawl and

index, use a robots.txt file.

- Off-Page Optimization:
    - Backlinks: Create high-quality backlinks from reputable industry websites. Prioritize quality over quantity.
    - Social Media: Participate in social media platforms to enhance brand visibility and maybe gain social signals, which can have an indirect impact on SEO.

- User Experience and Engagement:
    - Mobile Optimization: As a significant part of people access the internet via mobile devices, prioritize a flawless mobile experience.
    - User Engagement: Encourage user involvement, such as comments, shares, and reviews, because these signals can help SEO.

- Continuous Monitoring and Improvement:
    - Analytics: Track your website's performance, user behavior, and traffic sources with tools like Google Analytics.
    - Algorithm Updates: Keep up to date on changes to search engine algorithms and alter your strategy accordingly.

- Content Updates: Update and renew your content regularly to keep it relevant and valuable.

Stage 9: Sponsored Ads

9.a. PPC Ads

Pay-Per-Click (PPC) commercials are internet advertisements in which advertisers pay a fee each time their ad is clicked. It is a search engine marketing approach, such as Google AdWords, in which businesses bid for ad placement in a search engine's sponsored links when someone searches for a specific keyword. Advertisers only pay when a user clicks on their ad, directing targeted traffic to their website. PPC campaigns are a popular and successful approach for businesses to increase their online presence, traffic, and revenues.

How It Can Help Your Brand?

- Increased Visibility: PPC advertisements ensure that your brand appears near the top of search results, increasing visibility and brand familiarity among potential customers.

- Targeted Audience: You may target certain demographics, localities, and interests to ensure your adverts reach the intended audience and increase the likelihood of conversion.

- Cost-Effectiveness: Because you only pay when someone clicks on your ad, it is a low-cost advertising approach. You may create a budget, keep expenditures under control, and assess the performance of your initiatives.

- Immediate Results: In contrast to organic approaches, PPC yields immediate results. Your advertising can be live and drive visitors to your website within minutes.

- Measurable ROI: PPC solutions give precise data, allowing you to track the effectiveness of your advertisements. You can track click-through rates, conversions, and ROI, allowing you to make data-driven decisions about future campaigns.

- Brand Authority: Being at the top of search results increases the credibility and authority of your brand because users tend to trust and click on the first few results.

- Adaptability: Real-time adjustments can be made to PPC campaigns. If a specific keyword or ad content isn't doing well, you can change it right away, ensuring that your brand message is always optimized for the best results.

How To Do It?

- Set Clear Goals: Determine your goals for your PPC campaign, such as increasing website traffic, increasing sales, generating leads, or creating brand awareness.

- Keyword Research: Determine appropriate keywords for your products or services. To locate high-performing keywords with moderate search volume and competition, use tools like Google Keyword Planner.

- Create Compelling Ads: Create interesting ad copy that expresses your value offer effectively. To attract potential clients, highlight unique selling aspects, offers, or discounts. To boost clicks, use compelling language.

- Design Relevant Landing Pages: Make certain that your advertisements link consumers to unique, relevant landing pages on your website. These pages should be consistent with the content of the ad and give a smooth user experience. Improve the conversion rate of your landing pages.

- Set Budget and Bidding Strategy: Determine your campaign's daily or monthly budget. Based on your objectives and budget limits, select a bidding technique, such as manual CPC (Cost-Per-Click) or automatic bidding.

- Target Audience: Define your target audience by geography, age, gender, interests, and device type. Reduce your audience to target the most relevant users for your company.

- Ad Extensions: Ad extensions can be used to provide more information and increase clicks. Site links, callouts, and location extensions increase the visibility and relevancy of your ad.

- Monitor and Analyze: Monitor the performance of your campaign on a regular basis. Monitor data such as the click-through rate (CTR), conversion rate, and ROI. Use this information to discover successful techniques as well as areas for improvement.

- Optimize and Experiment: Optimize your campaigns on a regular basis. To determine the most efficient combinations, test numerous ad versions, keywords, and landing sites. Experiment with different options for ad scheduling and audience targeting.

- **Refine and Scale:** Refine your strategies based on the success of your campaign. Increase budget for high-performing advertisements and keywords while pausing or tweaking low-performing ones. Scaling your successful campaigns means reaching a larger audience.

- **A/B Testing:** A/B tests should be used to evaluate different ad elements (headlines, pictures, and calls-to-action) and discover which versions produce the best results. Use these insights to improve your ads.

- **Stay Updated:** PPC platforms, algorithms, and user habits are always evolving. Keep up to current on market changes, platform features, and best practices in order to adjust your plans accordingly.

9.b. Display Advertisements

Display advertisements are visual advertisements on websites and mobile applications to promote products, services, or brands. Display advertising, as opposed to text-based ads, contains graphics, videos, or interactive components, making them visually engaging to consumers. These advertisements, which can be static or dynamic, are strategically placed on websites that are relevant to the target population. Display adverts are an important component of Internet marketing efforts because they allow businesses to reach out to potential customers, raise brand awareness, and generate website traffic. Advertisers can target certain demographics, hobbies, and behaviors to ensure that their message reaches the correct audience and has the greatest impact and engagement.

How It Can Help Your Brand?

- Increased Visibility: Display advertising raises your brand's online visibility by appearing on relevant websites and reaching a larger audience, including prospective buyers who aren't actively searching for your products or services.

- Brand Awareness: Display advertising helps to enhance brand recognition by creatively exhibiting your brand through graphics. Consistent exposure to your brand message improves consumer recognition and familiarity.

- Targeted Audience: Display ads enable accurate demographic, interest, online behavior, and location targeting. This guarantees that your message is seen by the most relevant audience, boosting the possibility of viewers becoming customers.

- Drive Website Traffic: Display advertisements with appealing information and imagery can drive people to your website. This increased traffic might result in more interactions, such as product questions, purchases, or sign-ups, which can help your brand's online profile.

- Retargeting: Display advertisements allow for retargeting, which is a strong strategy that shows adverts to viewers who have previously visited your website. This reminder can entice potential clients who did not buy during their first visit to return, improving the odds of conversion.

- Engagement and Interaction: User involvement is encouraged via interactive display ads such as video commercials and interactive banners. Interactive components can increase click-through rates and improve user experiences, increasing the bond between your company and its audience.

- Measurable Results: Digital display advertising provides comprehensive analytics and metrics. You can measure the impact of your campaigns and make data-driven decisions to optimize your brand's marketing tactics by tracking impressions, clicks, conversions, and other key performance indicators.

How To Do It?

- **Define Your Goals:** Establish the goals of your display advertising strategy. Clear goals will guide your campaign strategy, whether it's raising website traffic, generating leads, or increasing sales.

- **Identify Your Target Audience:** Learn about your target audience's demographics, interests, and online behavior. This data aids in the creation of targeted and relevant advertisements that resonate with potential clients.

- **Design Compelling Creatives:** Make visually beautiful and engaging advertising creatives. Use high-quality graphics, attention-grabbing headlines, and brief, convincing writing. Consider including animations, movies, or interactive components in interactive advertising to increase user engagement.

- **Choose the Right Ad Formats:** Make visually beautiful and engaging advertising creatives. Use high-quality graphics, attention-grabbing headlines, and brief, convincing writing. Consider including animations, movies, or interactive components in interactive advertising to increase user engagement.

- Create Landing Pages: Create specific landing pages that correspond to your ad content. Maintain a consistent message and design throughout the transition from the ad to the landing page. Improve conversion rates by including clear calls-to-action and relevant content on the landing page.

- Set Up Ad Campaigns: To launch your campaign, select an advertising platform (such as Google Ads, Facebook Ads, or display ad networks). Establish your budget, targeting parameters, and timetable. Use the platform's targeting features to efficiently reach your target demographic.

- Monitor and Optimize: Monitor the performance of your campaign on a regular basis. Metrics like as impressions, clicks, click-through rates (CTR), and conversions should be tracked. Analyze the data to determine what works best and make any required changes. A/B testing various ad variations might aid in optimizing your adverts for better results.

- Implement Retargeting: Set up retargeting campaigns, if applicable, to re-engage users who have previously visited your website. Create targeted retargeting advertisements to remind consumers about your products or services and entice them to return and complete a desired action.

- Comply with Regulations: Adhere to advertising guidelines and regulations, such as privacy policies and data protection legislation, to guarantee your ads are lawful and deliver a great customer experience.

- Evaluate and Iterate: After the campaign has ended, compare the results to your initial objectives. Determine your successes and places for development. Make use of these information to improve your future display advertising efforts.

9.c. Social Media Advertising

Social media advertising is an effective digital marketing technique that entails producing and executing targeted advertisements on social media platforms such as Facebook, Instagram, Twitter, and LinkedIn. These advertisements are intended to reach certain demographics, raise brand awareness, and boost user interaction. Marketers use a variety of ad forms, such as photos, videos, and carousel advertising, to successfully communicate their messaging. Businesses can use social media advertising to engage with their target audience, promote products or services, and generate leads or purchases, eventually increasing brand visibility and revenue in the online arena.

How It Can Help Your Brand?

- Increased Brand Awareness: Social Media advertising allows you to reach a larger audience, enhancing the visibility of your business among potential customers.

- Targeted Audience Reach: Ads may be carefully targeted based on demographics, interests, geography, and activity, ensuring that your message reaches the intended audience.

- Higher Engagement: Ad formats that are engaging inspire visitors to interact with your content, resulting in more likes, shares, comments, and overall engagement.

- Lead Generation: Social media advertisements can direct traffic to your website or landing pages, capturing leads and potential consumers who are interested in your products or services.

- Boosted Website Traffic: Ads can help you improve the amount of visitors to your website, increasing the possibilities of conversions and purchases.

- Improved Sales and Revenue: Effective social media advertising can have a direct impact on sales by influencing users' purchasing decisions and motivating them to make purchases.

- Data Insights: Social media sites provide thorough data, allowing you to assess the effectiveness of your advertisements. These insights aid in the refinement of your plans for improved results.

- Competitive Advantage: A strong social media presence can set you apart from the competition by making your brand more memorable and identifiable to potential customers.

- **Cost-Effectiveness:** When compared to traditional advertising tactics, social media advertising is frequently less expensive, delivering substantial value for your marketing investment.

- **Real-time Feedback:** Social media platforms allow you to communicate directly with your target audience, allowing you to get immediate feedback, handle complaints, and enhance your products or services based on client feedback.

- **Global Reach:** Social media advertisements can reach a worldwide audience, boosting your brand's influence beyond geographic limits and offering up new markets and opportunities.

How To Do It?

- **Set Clear Goals:** Determine your goals for your social media advertising. Having specific objectives will guide your marketing strategy, whether it's raising website traffic, generating leads, increasing sales, or improving brand awareness.

- Know Your Audience: Understand the demographics, interests, behaviors, and preferences of your target audience. Use this data to develop highly targeted ads that will resonate with your target audience.

- Choose the Right Social Media Platforms: Choose the social media channels where your target demographic spends the most time. Popular options include Facebook, Instagram, Twitter, LinkedIn, and Pinterest. Each platform has its own audience and advertising formats.

- Create Compelling Content: Create eye-catching imagery, appealing writing, and a clear call-to-action (CTA) in your ad content. To keep your audience's interest, use high-quality graphics or videos.

- Set a Budget: Establish your advertising budget. Social media networks include a variety of budgeting choices, such as daily or lifetime budgets, as well as cost-per-click (CPC) or cost-per-impression (CPM) pricing methods. Begin with a low budget and gradually increase it based on campaign results.

- Define Targeting Parameters: To narrow down your audience, use the platform's targeting settings. Users can be targeted based on demographics, geography, interests, activities, and other factors. The more specific your targeting, the more effective your adverts will be.

- Create Custom Audiences: Upload your existing client list or website visitors to create custom audiences. This enables you to retarget people who have previously expressed interest in your business, boosting the possibility of conversions.

- Monitor and Optimize: Use the platform's analytics tools to track ad performance on a regular basis. Metrics like as click-through rates (CTR), conversion rates, and return on ad spend (ROAS) should be monitored. Optimize your advertising based on the data by modifying targeting, content, or budget to increase outcomes.

- A/B Testing: Experiment with different ad variations (pictures, wording, CTAs) to see what works best for your target demographic. A/B testing allows you to fine-tune your advertisements and maximize their efficacy.

- Ad Compliance and Guidelines: To ensure that your ads are accepted and displayed, follow each platform's advertising standards and policies. Ads that violate these restrictions may be rejected, and accounts may be fined.

- **Continuous Learning:** Keep up with the most recent social media advertising trends and best practices. Social media networks are always adding new features and capabilities that can help your advertising efforts.

- **Seek Professional Help if Needed:** If managing social media advertising is daunting, consider hiring a digital marketing agency or a social media advertising professional to enhance your campaigns.

9.d. Video Ads

Video ads are brief promotional videos designed to engage and grab the attention of the audience, and are often used to market products or services. These advertisements are intended to be visually appealing, with intriguing imagery, compelling stories, and pertinent themes. Video advertisements can be seen on a variety of platforms, such as social media, streaming services, and websites. They seek to successfully communicate a brand's message, raise brand awareness, and increase user engagement. With the rise of digital marketing, firms are using video commercials to reach a larger audience and leave a lasting impression on viewers, resulting in greater sales and brand loyalty.

How It Can Help Your Brand?

- **Increased Engagement:** Video content is more interesting and memorable than text or images, and it efficiently captures the audience's attention. Viewers are more likely to interact with and share video advertisements, increasing the reach of your business.
- **Enhanced Brand Awareness:** Engaging videos leave an indelible mark on viewers, increasing brand recall. When customers see your brand in intriguing video content on a regular basis, they become more familiar with your products or services.

- **Improved Conversions:** By presenting product features, benefits, and user testimonials, advertisements can influence purchasing decisions. Potential buyers can be persuaded by engaging storytelling and visually appealing material, resulting in increased conversion rates.

- **Better SEO Ranking:** Search engine results pages frequently favor websites having video content. Video advertisements can boost the SEO of your website, making it easier for potential clients to find your business online.

- Social Media Visibility: Video content is prioritized by social media networks, making it more likely to show in users' feeds. Through social media shares and likes, your brand can obtain recognition among a larger audience by developing shareable video commercials.

- Emotional Connection: Videos allow you to successfully elicit emotions, resulting in a deep connection with your audience. Emotional resonance increases brand loyalty and encourages customers to prefer your brand over competitors.

- Mobile-Friendly Content: With the growing popularity of smartphones, video adverts are now available to viewers on a variety of devices. Mobile-friendly films ensure that your brand's message reaches customers regardless of device.

- Detailed Analytics: You may track audience engagement, watch time, and demographics using the precise data provided by video platforms. Analyzing this data allows you to improve your marketing efforts.

<u>How To Do It?</u>

- Define Your Goals: Determine whether your video ad's goal is to raise brand awareness, drive sales, or promote a specific product/service. Your content creation is guided by certain aims.

- Know Your Audience: Learn about the preferences, interests, and demographics of your target audience. Make your video more relatable and engaging by tailoring it to their emotions and needs.

- Craft a Compelling Story: Create a story that captivates viewers from beginning to end. Tell a story that emotionally resonates with your audience, increasing their likelihood of remembering and engaging with your business.

- Focus on Visual Appeal: Use high-quality photographs, rich colors, and skilled editing to create visually engaging material. Visual aesthetics are critical in keeping viewers' attention.

- Keep it Concise: Because people's attention spans are short, make your video brief and to the point. Aim for a length that effectively conveys your message without losing the audience's attention—usually between 30 seconds and 2 minutes.

- Incorporate Branding: Integrate your brand aspects, such as your logo, colors, and tagline, into the video seamlessly. Brand consistency strengthens your identity and increases brand memory.

- Add Engaging Call-to-Actions (CTAs): Encourage visitors to perform particular activities such as visiting your website, purchasing something, or subscribing. Clear and enticing CTAs direct readers to the next step.

- Optimize for Mobile Devices: As a substantial part of viewers use smartphones, make sure your video is mobile-friendly. To ensure a smooth watching experience, test your movie on a variety of devices.

- Promote Across Platforms: Share your video advertisement on social media, YouTube, and your website. Use customized advertising to reach certain groups and maximize the effect of your video.

- Measure and Analyze: Analyze analytics such as views, engagement, and conversion rates once you've launched your video ad. Use these data to improve future efforts by learning what performs best for your target demographic.

9.e. Remarketing/Retargeting Ads

Remarketing, also known as retargeting, is a digital advertising approach that targets individuals who have previously visited a website or engaged with a brand online but did not buy or take the required action. It operates by tracking users' online behavior and displaying personalized advertisements to them across different websites and platforms they visit. These adverts serve as a reminder, prompting users to return to the website and complete the required activity, resulting in higher conversion rates and greater efficacy of online marketing efforts.

How It Can Help Your Brand?

- Increased Conversions: Remarketing encourages people who have previously shown interest to return to your website, boosting the possibility of conversions, whether it's making a purchase, signing up, or filling out a form.

- Enhanced ROI: Remarketing improves ad expenditure by targeting visitors who are more likely to interact with your business. This method maximizes ROI by directing resources toward re-engaging potential customers rather than wide, uninterested audiences.

- Improved Brand Recall: Seeing your brand across several platforms increases brand awareness and keeps your products or services fresh in the minds of your target audience, making them more inclined to consider your brand when making a purchase choice.

- Personalized Engagement: Remarketing enables you to personalize advertising based on previous experiences with people, adjusting the message and offerings to their tastes. Personalized content improves the user experience and develops a bond with your brand.

- Reduced Cart Abandonment: Remarketing helps e-commerce enterprises recover abandoned carts by reminding users of the things they left behind and urging them to complete the transaction.

- Data-driven Insights: Remarketing campaigns provide useful data and insights into user behavior, allowing you to fine-tune your marketing efforts. Analyzing this data allows for a better understanding of client preferences, allowing for more targeted and effective future advertising.

- Competitive Advantage: Effective remarketing gives your brand a competitive advantage. Engaging potential clients after they leave your site keeps your brand in their minds, making it less likely that they will be swayed by competitors' offerings.

How To Do It?

- Set Clear Goals: Set explicit goals, such as increasing sales, generating leads, or decreasing cart abandonment. Your remarketing campaign will be guided by certain objectives.

- Install Tracking Pixels: Remarketing tags or pixels should be integrated into your website. These code snippets monitor visitor behavior and allow you to generate audience segments depending on their activities.

- Segment Your Audience: Segment your audience depending on their activity, such as visitors who saw certain product pages, abandoned carts, or people who visited but did not interact.

- Create Compelling Ads: Create visually engaging and persuasive commercials for each audience segment. Customize your messaging to their individual needs, concerns, or interests to increase engagement.

- Choose the Right Platforms: For remarketing campaigns, use popular advertising platforms such as Google Ads, Facebook Ads, or other social media networks. These platforms include powerful remarketing options as well as a large audience reach.

- Set Budget and Bidding Strategy: Set a budget for your remarketing campaign and choose a bidding strategy based on your goals and financial limits, such as cost per click (CPC) or cost per thousand impressions (CPM).

- Monitor and Optimize: Monitor the performance of your remarketing advertising on a regular basis. Consider indicators like as click-through rates, conversion rates, and return on ad spend (ROAS). Use this information to optimize your advertisements, concentrating on what works best for different audience categories.

- Experiment and A/B Test: To determine the most effective combinations, test various ad formats, creatives, and messaging. A/B testing allows you to fine-tune your remarketing strategy and invest in what produces the best results.

- Comply with Privacy Regulations: Ensure that privacy rules such as GDPR or CCPA are followed. To maintain trust and legal compliance, obtain user consent where appropriate and respect users' privacy preferences.

Stage 10: Building Loyal Customer's

10.a. Chatbot Whatsapp/Web

WhatsApp Web is a tool that allows users to see their WhatsApp messages and communicate with contacts from their computer's web browser. It provides a handy way to send and receive messages, photographs, videos, and documents from a computer by syncing the user's phone with the web interface. While WhatsApp Web is not a chatbot, developers can construct chatbots that are integrated with WhatsApp to automate chats and deliver various services, improving user experience and communication efficiency.

How It Can Help Your Brand?

- Enhanced Customer Engagement: A WhatsApp chatbot enables your brand to interact with clients in real-time, offering rapid solutions to concerns and thereby increasing customer happiness and loyalty.

- 24/7 Support: Chatbots can provide round-the-clock customer care, guaranteeing that clients can access help at any time, including beyond typical business hours, resulting in better customer service.

- Cost-Efficiency: Chatbots automate consumer interactions, reducing the need for human agents to address repetitive requests, resulting in cost savings for your company.

- Personalized Interactions: Chatbots can collect data and provide customers with personalized recommendations, promotions, and content, boosting their experience and driving sales.

- Order Processing: Chatbots can help clients place orders, track shipments, and provide order-related information, expediting and optimizing the purchasing experience.

- Feedback and Surveys: Chatbots may collect feedback and perform surveys, allowing your brand to gain vital insights into consumer happiness and preferences while also assisting in product/service enhancements.

- Lead Generation: Chatbots can collect important information and qualify leads by communicating with potential customers, helping to your brand's sales and marketing efforts.

How To Do It?
- Understand Your Audience and Goals: Determine your target audience and the goal of your chatbot. Determine which jobs you want the chatbot to undertake and which problems you want it to address for your consumers.

- Choose a Chatbot Platform: Choose a chatbot development platform that allows for WhatsApp integration. Dialogflow, Microsoft

Bot Framework, and custom solutions written in programming languages such as Python or Node.js are examples of popular systems.

- **Create Your Chatbot:** Create the conversational flow, responses, and interactions for your chatbot. Use natural language processing (NLP) to effectively interpret and reply to user requests. Add features that are relevant to your objectives, such as answering FAQs, processing orders, or providing personalized recommendations.

- **Set Up WhatsApp Business API:** You must utilize the WhatsApp Business API to integrate your chatbot with WhatsApp. Apply for API access through the official WhatsApp Business page. Once authorized, you will be sent the credentials and documentation needed to set up your WhatsApp Business account.

- **Develop Integration Code:** Code should be written to link your chatbot to the WhatsApp Business API. This connection code connects your chatbot platform to WhatsApp. To build message-sending, receiving, and processing functionality, follow the API guidelines supplied by WhatsApp.

- **Host Your Chatbot:** Deploy your chatbot on a server or cloud platform so that it can respond to incoming messages in real-time. Ascertain that the server is secure, dependable, and capable of handling the anticipated load.

- **Test and Iterate:** Test your chatbot thoroughly to find and resolve any bugs. Conduct user testing to collect input and make required changes to improve the user experience.

- **Launch and Monitor:** When you're satisfied with your chatbot's performance, make it available to the public. To assess its performance, keep track of its interactions, examine user input, and track critical data. Update and enhance the chatbot regularly based on user interactions and feedback.

10.b. Loyalty programme

A loyalty program is a marketing technique that uses rewards or incentives to encourage customers to make repeat purchases or engage with a business. These programs reward participants with points, miles, or other types of currency based on their spending or interaction levels. These accrued incentives can subsequently be used for discounts, free items, exclusive access, or other benefits, thereby increasing customer loyalty and retention. Loyalty programs not only deliver concrete rewards to customers but also foster a sense of belonging and recognition, boosting their whole experience and building their bond with the brand.

How It Can Help Your Brand?

- Customer Retention: Loyalty programs encourage repeat purchases, resulting in higher customer retention rates. Customers who have previously purchased from your brand are more inclined to do so again, increasing long-term profitability.

- Increased Revenue: Customers who are happy and loyal likely to spend more money. By providing rewards, you incentivize customers to spend more to gain points, resulting in increased sales and revenue for your company.

- Brand Advocacy: Customers who are loyal to your brand are more inclined to promote it to others. Positive word-of-mouth generated by delighted loyalty program participants can attract new consumers, thereby increasing your customer base.

- Data Collection: Loyalty programs enable you to gather vital client information such as purchase history and preferences. By analyzing this data, you can tailor your marketing activities, increasing client engagement and satisfaction.

- Competitive Advantage: A well-executed loyalty program distinguishes your brand from competition. Because of the added value provided by loyalty benefits, customers are more inclined to choose your brand over rivals offering identical products or services.

- Customer Engagement: Loyalty programs allow for meaningful engagement with customers. Customers feel valued and connected with your company when they receive exclusive deals, personalized communications, and unique access.

- Feedback Loop: Loyalty program participants that are engaged are more likely to submit feedback. Their insights can assist you in better understanding customer preferences, allowing you to adapt and improve your products, resulting in increased customer happiness.

How To Do It?

- Define Objectives: Outline your objectives, whether they be to increase customer retention, increase revenue, or collect customer data. The framework of your program will be determined by your objectives.

- Know Your Audience: Understand your target audience's interests and behaviors in order to create rewards that will appeal to them and increase their motivation to engage.

- Choose the Right Rewards: Provide appealing incentives like discounts, free products, exclusive access, or tailored experiences. Make certain that the rewards are valuable and relevant to your clients.

- Simplicity is Key: Keep the program simple and straightforward. Complex systems can deter involvement. Explain in detail how customers can earn and redeem incentives.

- Leverage Technology: Track consumer behaviors, manage points, and automate interactions with loyalty program software. Technology simplifies the process, making it more convenient for both you and your consumers.

- **Promote Your Program:** Market your loyalty program aggressively through numerous sources. To raise awareness and drive sign-ups, use email marketing, social media, and in-store promotions.

- **Provide Exceptional Service:** Excellent customer service increases loyalty. Ensure that your personnel is properly trained to handle program-related inquiries and issues in a timely and professional manner.

- **Track and Analyze Data:** Analyze customer data on a regular basis to determine program effectiveness. Determine trends, preferences, and areas for improvement to make data-driven decisions.

- **Encourage Engagement:** Communicate with members on a regular basis, delivering personalized bargains and exclusive updates. Engage with them through surveys or feedback systems to continuously improve their experience.

- **Adapt and Innovate:** Maintain your adaptability. To keep your loyalty program fresh and engaging over time, keep an eye on industry developments and client feedback.

10.c. CRM

Customer Relationship Management (CRM) is a company strategy centered on tracking and analyzing interactions with present and prospective customers. It makes use of technology to organize, automate, and synchronize sales, marketing, customer service, and technical support activities, resulting in increased customer satisfaction and loyalty. CRM solutions enable businesses to strengthen relationships, increase sales, and optimize marketing efforts by streamlining communication, tracking customer interactions, managing prospects, and analyzing data.

How It Can Help Your Brand?

- Enhanced Customer Relationships: CRM enables individualized interactions by understanding consumer preferences and behavior. This builds trust and loyalty, which improves the whole consumer experience.

- Improved Customer Service: Support staff can give faster and more accurate assistance if they have access to client data. Resolving problems as soon as possible enhances customer happiness and loyalty.

- Efficient Marketing: CRM systems provide segmented marketing campaigns based on consumer preferences and segmentation. This precision improves conversion rates while also optimizing marketing resources.

- Sales Growth: CRM aids in lead management, sales forecasting, and opportunity monitoring by automating sales operations. This simplified strategy boosts sales efficiency and income.

- Data-driven Decisions: Through data analysis, CRM gives useful insights. Brands may improve their competitiveness by making informed judgments about product development, pricing tactics, and market expansion.

- Customer Retention: CRM identifies at-risk clients and enables proactive efforts to keep them. Customers that are satisfied and loyal not only earn repeat business but also become brand evangelists.

- Streamlined Communication: CRM centralizes communication, ensuring that messaging is consistent across all channels. This uniformity reinforces brand identification and increases client trust.

- Competitive Advantage: CRM-enabled brands respond quickly to market developments, giving them a competitive advantage. Understanding client wants and market trends allows you to stay ahead of the competition.

- Feedback Utilization: CRM systems collect consumer input, allowing brands to address issues and improve products or services, resulting in improved levels of customer satisfaction.
- Long-term Growth: CRM aids to long-term growth by fostering customer relationships. Customers that are satisfied stay loyal, suggest others, and contribute considerably to a brand's long-term success.

How To Do It?

- Define Your Objectives: Clearly define your CRM implementation goals, whether they are to improve customer service, increase revenue, or streamline marketing operations.

- Choose the Right CRM Software: Investigate and select a CRM solution that meets your company's needs and budget. Consider things like scalability, usability, and integration capabilities.

- Data Migration and Integration: Collect and move existing customer data from diverse sources to the CRM platform. Ensure that other critical systems, like as email, marketing, and sales tools, are seamlessly integrated.

- Customization: Collect and move existing customer data from diverse sources to the CRM platform. Ensure that other critical systems, like as email, marketing, and sales tools, are seamlessly integrated.

- User Training: To properly use the CRM system, thoroughly train your personnel. Provide continuing assistance and resources to resolve concerns and challenges, allowing the team to reach its full potential.

- Data Quality Management: To ensure accuracy, update and sanitize the data in the CRM on a regular basis. To avoid duplicates and errors, implement data validation rules and routines.

- Automate Processes: Repetitive tasks, like as follow-up emails and lead assignments, can be automated. Workflow automation improves efficiency, allowing your staff to concentrate on high-value tasks.

- Monitor and Analyze: To acquire insights into customer behavior, sales trends, and marketing performance, use the CRM's reporting and analytics features. Monitor critical KPIs to determine the CRM's influence on your business goals.

- Feedback and Iteration: Collect user input on the functioning and user experience of the CRM system. Iterate and upgrade the CRM on a regular basis based on user feedback and changing business demands.

- Encourage Adoption: Create a CRM culture within your firm. To encourage personnel and ensure widespread adoption and maximize the system's potential impact, highlight success stories and benefits.

10.d. Personalized Marketing

Personalized marketing is a marketing technique that targets individual consumers based on their interests, activities, and demographics. It uses data analysis and technology to deliver personalized information, product recommendations, and offers to customers, resulting in a more relevant and engaging experience. Businesses may develop stronger connections, increase customer happiness, and drive sales by understanding specific consumer requirements and interests. Personalized marketing increases consumer loyalty by demonstrating that firms recognize their uniqueness, resulting in increased customer retention and business growth.

<u>How It Can Help Your Brand?</u>

- **Improved Customer Experience:** Personalization improves the overall customer experience by making interactions more relevant and engaging. Customers feel cherished and understood when they are catered to individually, which leads to higher satisfaction.

- **Higher Customer Engagement:** Tailored content and product recommendations draw customers in and encourage them to interact with your company. Interactive and personalized marketing efforts are more likely to be shared, increasing the reach of your business via word-of-mouth and social media.

- **Increased Conversion Rates:** Customers are more inclined to buy when they receive individualized offers or recommendations. Marketing communications that are tailored to their interests and requirements result in higher conversion rates, which drive sales and revenue.

- Enhanced Customer Loyalty: Customers develop a sense of loyalty as a result of personalized encounters. They are more likely to remain loyal to your company, making repeat purchases and becoming brand ambassadors if they feel understood and appreciated.

- Data-driven Insights: Data analysis is used in personalized marketing to provide useful insights into client behavior and preferences. These insights assist you in making educated decisions, refining your marketing strategy, and adapting your offers to match changing customer needs.

- Competitive Advantage: Brands that use individualized marketing effectively acquire a competitive advantage. Understanding your clients better than your competition enables you to provide greater, targeted experiences, thereby distinguishing your brand in the market.

- Customer Retention: Long-term partnerships are fostered by personalized marketing. You can keep existing clients by consistently responding to their preferences and input, lowering churn rates, and assuring a steady customer base.

How To Do It?

- Collect and Analyze Data: Collect information from a variety of sources, such as website interactions, purchase histories, social media, and surveys. Analyze this data using analytics tools to find patterns, preferences, and behaviors among your customers.

- Segment Your Audience: Segment your consumer base based on demographics, activities, or interests. To enable focused marketing activities, each group should have distinct features.

- Create Detailed Customer Profiles: Create extensive profiles for each segment that outline their preferences, requirements, and issues. Learn about their purchasing process and customize your marketing messaging accordingly.

- Implement Personalized Content: Create customized content such as product recommendations, emails, and website messaging. Use dynamic content technologies to personalize messages based on user preferences, geography, or previous interactions.

- Utilize Marketing Automation: Use marketing automation solutions to send targeted messages at the appropriate moment. To engage customers based on their behaviors and interactions, automate email campaigns, product recommendations, and social media posts.

- Personalize Product Recommendations: Use recommendation engines to evaluate consumer behavior and recommend products or services that they are likely to be interested in. This increases the likelihood of cross-selling and upselling.

- Optimize User Experience: Make your website and mobile apps more personalized for users. Enhance user engagement by implementing features such as personalized landing pages, product suggestions, and customized navigation pathways.

- A/B Testing and Optimization: A/B tests tailored marketing initiatives on a regular basis to determine their performance. Use the results to fine-tune your plans by determining what resonates most with various customer categories.

- Respect Customer Privacy: Ensure that data protection regulations are followed and that consumer privacy is respected. To develop trust, obtain explicit authorization for data gathering and explicitly disclose how customer data will be utilized.

- Monitor and Adapt: Monitor the effectiveness of tailored marketing strategies on a regular basis. Analyze client feedback and modify your plans in response to shifting market trends and customer preferences.

<u>Ecommerce Checkpoints:</u>

1. Keep Payment mode Safe & Secure

Secure payment is the practice of protecting financial transactions made over the Internet or other electronic channels from unauthorized access, fraud, and data breaches. It entails using encryption, authentication procedures, and secure networks to protect sensitive information like credit card numbers and personal identifiers. Businesses and customers can engage in online transactions with confidence by establishing strong security measures, lowering the chance of financial loss, and preventing sensitive data from getting into the hands of hackers.

How It Can Help Your Brand?

- Builds Trust: Secure payment methods instill trust in clients, who are more inclined to make purchases when they believe their financial information is secure.

- Enhances Reputation: A reputation for safe transactions improves the image of your brand, attracting more customers and promoting repeat business.

- Reduces Chargebacks: Secure payment methods can aid in the reduction of chargeback disputes, saving your company money while preserving great client connections.

- Boosts Customer Confidence: Customers are more likely to give personal information when they know their data is secure, allowing your business to tailor services and marketing and increasing customer happiness.

- Encourages Global Expansion: Secure payment solutions promote international transactions, allowing your business to access a worldwide audience and grow its market reach.

- Compliance and Legal Protection: Adhering to safe payment standards assures regulatory compliance, shielding your business from legal concerns and financial fines.

- Fosters Customer Loyalty: Providing a secure payment experience increases customer loyalty because customers are more likely to return to a platform where they believe their transactions are safe and their data is secure.

- Reduces Abandoned Carts: Secure payment options reduce the likelihood of cart abandonment, ensuring that potential customers complete their transactions and thereby improving your sales revenue.

- Enhances User Experience: A smooth and secure payment procedure contributes to a great user experience, which leads to higher customer satisfaction and positive evaluations, increasing the reputation of your brand.

- Differentiation: Using your brand's safe payment options to separate yourself from competitors gives clients a compelling incentive to prefer your services over others.

How To Do It?

- **Use SSL Encryption:** SSL (Secure Sockets Layer) encryption protects your website. SSL encrypts data sent between a web server and a user's browser, making it impossible to eavesdrop or tamper with.

- **Choose a Secure Payment Gateway:** Choose a trustworthy payment gateway firm that adheres to industry norms and laws. PayPal, Stripe, and Authorize.Net are all popular possibilities. Payment transactions are handled securely by these gateways.

- **Comply with PCI DSS:** Ensure that the Payment Card Industry Data Security Standard (PCI DSS) criteria are met. This collection of security standards is intended to safeguard cardholder information during payment transactions. Following PCI DSS requirements is critical for secure payment processing.

- **Implement Two-Factor Authentication:** Enforce two-factor authentication for user accounts to add an additional layer of security beyond passwords. This aids in the prevention of illegal access to sensitive consumer data.

- **Regular Security Audits:** Perform frequent security audits and vulnerability assessments to discover and address possible system flaws. Regular testing guarantees that your security measures are still effective in the long run.

- **Tokenization:** Tokenization, a process that substitutes sensitive data with unique tokens, should be implemented. Even if a hacker gains access to your database, they will not be able to retrieve useable credit card information, hence increasing security.

- **Update Software:** Maintain the most recent versions of your website platform, plugins, and payment gateway software. Security patches that correct known vulnerabilities are frequently included in software updates.

- **Monitor Transactions:** Keep an eye out for strange patterns or activity in transactions. Install real-time monitoring systems to detect and respond to questionable activity as soon as possible.

- **Data Backups:** Backup client data and payment information on a regular basis. In the event of a security compromise, having backup data means that you can quickly restore services without losing essential data.

- **Customer Communication:** Customers should be informed about the security precautions you have in place. Transparent communication boosts brand trust and confidence.

- **Work with Security Experts:** Consider collaborating with cybersecurity pros who specialize in secure online payment systems if you lack in-house experience. They can offer customized solutions depending on your unique needs and hazards.

2. Instant Chat Option

The term "chat options" refers to the range of features and capabilities that can be found in chat platforms or programs to improve communication. Text-based messaging, voice communications, video calls, and multimedia sharing (including images and videos) are examples of these alternatives. To further convey emotions graphically, chat choices frequently include GIFs, stickers, and emoticons. Additionally, a lot of platforms allow for group chats, which let several people take part in a discussion at once. Functionalities such as read receipts serve as indicators of message viewing, and typing indicators signal the process of creating a response.

How It Can Help Your Brand?

- Chat options allow for direct consumer engagement, allowing for personalized service, real-time conversations, and quick answers to questions, all of which contribute to the development of stronger customer relationships.

- Chat platforms provide round-the-clock assistance, quickly resolving client concerns. This boosts consumer happiness and loyalty and improves the reputation of your brand.

- Routine inquiries can be handled by automated chatbots, which eliminates the need for large customer care personnel and saves money without sacrificing effectiveness.

- Use chats to interact with customers and get insightful feedback that will help you develop your product or service and gain a deeper understanding of their requirements and preferences.

- Businesses can boost sales and conversion rates by offering rapid product information, addressing consumer problems, and assisting with purchase decisions using chat alternatives.

- By showcasing their personality, tone, and beliefs through conversations, brands can establish a distinctive identity that connects with consumers and fosters brand loyalty and emotional ties.

- Geographical boundaries are removed by chat options, which connect your business with a worldwide audience and increase your market reach and prospective clientele.

How To Do It?

- Choose the Right Platform: Choose messaging apps or chat platforms that make sense for your target market. Website chat widgets, WhatsApp, and Facebook Messenger are popular choices.

- Set Up Automated Responses: Create chatbots that can respond instantly to frequently asked questions, freeing up human resources for more complicated problems. Make sure these bots are properly trained and provide useful, pertinent information.

- Personalize Interactions: To give consumers a sense of value, personalize automated responses and interactions. Make use of their identities, provide tailored advice, and adjust your comments according to how they have previously interacted with your business.

- Train Support Staff: If human agents are used, be sure they have received adequate training in problem-solving techniques, product expertise, and customer service etiquette. It's essential to communicate politely and consistently.

- Integrate CRM Systems: Customer relationship management (CRM) systems can be integrated with chat options to monitor customer interactions, preferences, and past purchases. Marketing plans and customized interactions can be informed by this data.

- Implement Security Measures: Prioritize security when managing sensitive data. To safeguard client information and guarantee secure transactions, use end-to-end encryption and other security measures.

- Encourage Feedback: Invite individuals to share their opinions about their chat encounters. Utilize this input to continuously enhance your chat services.

- Monitor and Analyze: Keep an eye on chat conversations, examine client behavior, and evaluate how useful your chat features are. Determine trends, frequently asked questions and areas that need work.

- Iterate and Improve: Make the appropriate adjustments in light of the analysis. This could entail improving staff training, fine-tuning automatic responses, or adding new features to improve user experience.
- Promote Your Chat Services: Promote your chat options aggressively using a range of marketing platforms. Customers should be encouraged to use the chat feature for questions, help, and comments.

3. Social eCommerce and Marketplace

When social networking and online shopping are combined, users can browse, share, and buy things straight from social media platforms. This is known as social commerce. It makes use of social networks to make purchasing and selling easier, giving customers access to product recommendations, reviews, and influencers.

Conversely, a marketplace is an online venue where numerous vendors provide an array of goods or services, forming a single point of contact for consumers. These ideas are combined in social commerce within marketplaces, which creates a dynamic and engaging shopping environment by enabling users to shop, engage, and make purchases all within their social media experience.

How It Can Help Your Brand?

- Increased Visibility: By utilizing social media channels, social commerce increases the visibility of your business and makes your products visible to a larger market.

- Enhanced Engagement: Direct consumer interaction on social media promotes relationships, loyalty, and trust, all of which promote repeat business and goodwill.

- Targeted Advertising: Social media systems gather information, making it possible for tailored advertisements to target particular demographics and guaranteeing that prospective buyers who are most likely to make a purchase see your offerings.

- Influencer Partnerships: Through sincere recommendations, working with influencers in social commerce can boost sales, strengthen your brand's messaging, and establish your trust.

- Seamless Shopping Experience: Customers may explore products and make purchases more easily by using social commerce platforms, which provide a streamlined and convenient purchasing experience within their preferred social media apps.

- Real-time Feedback: Instant feedback and reviews are possible with social commerce, giving you the chance to highlight positive experiences, respond quickly to complaints, and enhance your goods and services in response to user feedback.

- Data Insights: Social media platforms offer useful analytics and data that let you comprehend consumer behavior, tastes, and trends. This helps you make data-driven judgments about your marketing tactics.

- Brand Loyalty Programs: By integrating loyalty programs into social commerce platforms, you can reward customers for their loyalty and entice them to interact with your business more by creating an incentive for repeat purchases.

- Competitive Advantage: Adopting social commerce offers your company a competitive edge, enabling you to keep ahead of the always-changing digital marketplace and adjust to shifting consumer preferences.

How To Do It?

- Choose the Right Platform: Determine which social media channels your target market is most engaged on. TikTok, Facebook, Pinterest, and Instagram are among the well-liked options.

- Create a Business Profile: Create a special business account on the platform(s) of your choice. Add correct details to your profile, such as a catchy bio, contact information, and a link to your website or online store.

- Develop High-Quality Content: Make eye-catching images, movies, and graphics to highlight your merchandise. If at all possible, spend money on expert photography and filming. Emphasize the advantages, features, and special selling factors of the product.

- Leverage Influencers: Join forces with influencers in your niche. Influencers can increase the visibility and credibility of your items by promoting them to their following. Make sure your brand's ideals are shared by the influencers.
- Enable Shopping Features: Make use of the shopping options available on the platform, such as Instagram Shopping, to tag products directly in posts so that customers can easily click and make purchases.

- Implement Secure Payment Gateways:To ensure safe transactions, set up secure payment gateways. Choose reputable payment processors to create trust in your customers.

- Provide Excellent Customer Service: Respond to consumer inquiries, comments, and messages as soon as possible. To improve the user experience and develop trust, provide great customer service.

- Run Targeted Ads: Use the social media networks' targeted advertising tools. Create visually stunning adverts that will entice your target audience to visit your online store.

- Monitor Analytics: Analyze social media insights and website statistics on a regular basis to evaluate the success of your social commerce operations. Change your plans in response to customer engagement and sales statistics.

- Optimize for Mobile Devices: Because many people access social media via smartphones and tablets, make sure your social commerce operations are mobile-friendly.

- Stay Updated: The features of social networking sites are often updated. Keep up to date on these developments and adjust your social commerce strategies accordingly to maximize your brand's reach and influence.